ECSTASY AND EXPERIENCES

A MYSTICAL JOURNEY

BY
SADHU VASWANI

Foreword by **Dada J. P. Vaswani**
Translation by **Aruna Jethwani**

Sterling Paperbacks

BOOKS ON SADHU VASWANI

English:
1. Sadhu Vaswani : His Life And Teachings – by J. P. Vaswani
2. He Walked With God – by J. P. Vaswani
3. Kindle The Light – by J. P. Vaswani
4. A Saint Of Our Times – by H. P. Vaswani
5. A Study Of T. L. Vaswani's Works – by Dr. R. M. Godhwani

Hindi:
1. Sadhu Vaswani : Unkaa Jeevan Aur Shikshaayen

Marathi:
1. Sadhu Vaswani – by Dr. Sharadchandra Kopidkar

BOOKS BY SADHU VASWANI

Breakfast With God
Discover Yourself!
Lights From Many Lanterns
Nuri Granth (Vol. 1) English
Nuri Granth (Vol. 2) English
Nuri Granth (Vol. 3) English
Nuri Granth (Vol. 4) English
Pilgrimage To God
Sufi Saints of East & West
The Bhagavad Gita: The Song of Life (With Sanskrit Slokas)
The Bhagavad Gita: The Song of The Supreme
The Heart of The Gita
The Life Beautiful
Thus Have I Learnt
Saint Mira
The Call of Mira Education
Gita : A Bible of Humanity
Krishna: The Saviour
The Call of New Education
Pearls of Great Price
Sind and the Sindhis
Prophets and Patriots

BOOKS BY SADHU VASWANI

Guru Nanak: Prophet of Peace
Kindle the Light
Golden Gleanings
Masters and Mystics
Heroes of History
The Voice of Vaswani

In Hindi
Satpurusho Ke Sakshi
Brindavan Ka Balak

Devnagri
Nuri Granth

In Marathi
Vaswani Vachnamirth
Mangalmay Jeev Sakal

Contents

Foreword — vii
Preface — xv
Translator's note — xix

Part-I

The Journey of Life Begins	2
In Calcutta—9, Chidamodi Lane	40
- At the feet of the Master	40
- In Calcutta	73
The European Tour	78

Part-II

Lahore Longing	130
Ecstasy of Mystics	146
Ways of a Wanderer	196
After the Partition in India	241
- The Night of Awakening/Enlightment	252
Death Song	258

STERLING PAPERBACKS
An imprint of
Sterling Publishers (P) Ltd.
A-59, Okhla Industrial Area, Phase-II,
New Delhi-110020.
Tel: 26387070, 26386209; Fax: 91-11-26383788
E-mail: mail@sterlingpublishers.com
www.sterlingpublishers.com

Ecstasy and Experiences: A Mystical Journey
© 2011, Sadhu Vaswani
ISBN 978 81 207 5818 6

All rights are reserved.
No part of this publication may be reproduced, stored in a retrieval system or transmitted, in any form or by any means, mechanical, photocopying, recording or otherwise, without prior written permission of the Sadhu Vaswani Mission.

Printed in India
Printed and Published by Sterling Publishers Pvt. Ltd.,
New Delhi-110 020.

Foreword

Our dear sister, Mrs. Aruna Jethwani, has brought out a beautiful English translation of Gurudev Sadhu Vaswani's autobiographical account, published earlier in Sindhi as, "*Dada Vaswani: Sandas-e Shabdan Mein*".

When I use the word 'autobiography' I do so with reservations: for nowadays, autobiographies are often attempts at self-glorification – of course, with certain notable exceptions. You would expect that the man who writes the autobiography would emerge as the 'hero' of his own account. Just a few pages of *Ecstasy and Experiences* will reveal that this book is an autobiography with a difference. If there is a 'hero' here, it is not the writer of the account; it is the Beloved, The One and Only Fair, the Hidden One whom we, with our worldly senses can never grasp. Who is the true Hero – The One whom Gurudev Sadhu Vaswani seeks to behold, to attain, to lose himself in!

May I tell you, you are not likely to come across such an account often! For years, the devotees of the Master have read the pages of the original Sindhi version to recapture the radiance, warmth and the brilliant spiritual effulgence of the great saint whom we humbly call our Gurudev; and yet, even the opening pages reveal to the reader, that this great saint of God was in quest of His true Self – his true identity.

Who am I? Whither is my home? Why do I wander here upon this earth?

These are the questions that echo and re-echo through the pages of this book. The reader has to be in tune with the frequency of the *atman*, the spirit, if he is to reap the real benefit of this extraordinary story of a mystic visionary's search for his true identity. You will be disappointed if you look for mundane details, statistics and a 'calendar of events' as we call them. But if you wish to catch a glimpse of the beauty, the inspiration that a true saint's life has to offer, you will certainly not be disappointed!

It is only the most fortunate amongst us, who are so blessed as to come in contact with a living saint, who brings about a transformation in our lives. Even after the briefest contact with them, we find that our very way of thinking has changed! Gurudev Sadhu Vaswani was such a saint, who brought about a transformation – nay, a spiritual revolution, in the lives of many people. He touched our hearts and souls with the power of his love, and showed us a glimpse of the beautiful world of the spirit, which we cannot hope to reach without the grace of a Guru.

We called him Gurudev; we called him a sufi *dervish*; we called him an *avatara purusha*; we called him an Angel of Compassion, a Messiah of the Lord. By the time he was fifty, he was known across the length and breadth of India as Sadhu Vaswani. But in his characteristic humility, he said, "I am not a *Sadhu*. I do but aspire to be a servant of the *sadhus*, the *rishis* and the saints."

Tributes were paid to him by men and women of light and leading in East and West. In the West, they spoke of him as a *Herald of the New Age*, a *Faraday of Spiritual Science*, a *Pioneer* and a *Path-Pointer*. The Irish poet, Dr. Cousins, saluted him as, "India's modern mystic," and a, "Forerunner of the New Age….a Thinker and Revealer of the deep truths of the Spirit." But he said, "I know not much. I only know that the longing within me grows, day by day, to be consumed, more and more, in the Flame of Sacrifice to Him, whose Beauty blooms in all the worlds and whose Love I see shinning, shinning everywhere!"

"By what name may we call you, Beloved of our hearts?" we asked him once. "May we call you a Sadhu, a guru, a yogi, a rishi? Or may we call you *Sache Patshah*, for you are, verily, the uncrowned king of our hearts?"

In answer, he said to us, "Call me by this simple name – Dada. For, I am your brother on the journey of life."

During the last years of his earth-pilgrimage, crowds followed him wherever he went; eager to touch the hem of his garment; thirsty souls yearned to see him and listen to his words of wisdom – more precious to them than pearls and rubies. But he gave himself no supernatural airs! He was one of the humblest of men that ever trod this earth. In him we beheld that rare humility of one who had reduced himself to nought. To use his own words, "I am a zero." Not the Arabic zero, which is a little circle that occupies space, but a Sindhi zero, which is nothing more than a little point! Having everything, he chose to live as a *fakir* – a man who possessed nothing! Knowing everything, he lived as one who knew nothing! His humility was profound – and it adorned him as a priceless jewel even in his utter simplicity.

He never claimed to be more than a brother. Many regarded him as their Master, their Guru. But he said, "I am a Guru of none. I am a disciple of all!"

It is said that saints and spiritual leaders must be wary of one besetting weakness – holy pride, or the feeling of superior sanctity that arises when thousands of devotees, disciples, admirers and followers offer their reverence to one in whom they behold God's Image.

Sadhu Vaswani was completely and utterly free from such pride. Indeed, he was they very personification of true humility. Once, a deputation of friends and admirers waited on Sadhu Vaswani, with a request that he write his autobiography.

"Your life is radiant with the light of wisdom and rich in experiences known only to you," they pleaded. "We beg you to share them with us and let hundreds and thousands benefit by your spiritual aspirations and achievements."

Can you guess what his reply was? This great sage who had been a brilliant scholar, a popular professor, a distinguished principal, a revered saint, a great educationalist, mystic visionary and philosopher admired and loved by the best of his contemporaries, smiled and answered: "There have been no achievements. The story of my life is a story of my abject poverty and God's abounding grace."

At the age of thirty, he had been invited to address the World Congress of Religions. Between the age of thirty and forty, he had been invited to become the Principal of some of the best colleges in North Western India. Gurudev Rabindranath Tagore, Pandit Madan Mohan Malaviya and Sarvepalli Radhakrishnan knew him and admired him. Mahatma Gandhi, Pandit Nehru, Acharya Kripalani and other eminent leaders visited his Shakti Ashram to pay their respects to this great son of India. And yet he said to us, "There have been no achievements…"

"To write an autobiography is to puff up one's ego!" he would say. "Such writing will bless neither him who writes nor him who reads."

He added, "If it is absolutely necessary to write an autobiography, let it be written after the pattern of St. Augustine's *Confessions*."

If you are wondering how this book came to be in your hands, let me tell you, it was transcribed from informal talks and *ruh-rihans* in the *satsang*, when devotees begged the Master to tell them something of his early life, when they were not privileged to know him. To many of us in those days, his every word was a treasure. "*Dada Vaswani: Sandas-e Shabdan Mein*", was thus a labour of love and devotion, compiled by eager aspirants who wished to preserve and cherish every precious event, memory and reflection that their Gurudev chose to share with them, in his love, magnanimity and grace.

Till now, this remarkable personal account of Gurudev Sadhu Vaswani's life was accessible only to those who could read and understand the lyrical Sindhi language. Our heartfelt appreciation must be expressed for Mrs. Aruna Jethwani who has taken painstaking efforts to prepare a translation which can reach more people with the inspiring message of the Master.

Mrs. Jethwani is a gifted writer, proficient in both her mother-tongue Sindhi, as well as in the English language – a rare gift these days! To her considerable talent as a poet and creative writer, she also adds the rare quality of devotion and reverence for the Master, who was well-known to her and her family, since her childhood. Therefore, it is no surprise that she brings into her translation qualities of head and heart that have enabled to achieve a fine balance between the Master's mystic vision and melodious language, even while being true to the letter and spirit of the original Sindhi discourse. Indeed, now many devotees of the Master would be grateful to Mrs. Jethwani for making this translation available to them! May Gurudev's choicest blessings be showered upon her!

Great was Gurudev's spiritual power; profound was his intellectual prowess; rich, his knowledge, wisdom and insight into life and the higher things of life. But his true sphere was the realm of the *atman*, the spirit. Living in the midst of humanity, he lived as one apart, for he lived in the world of the *atman*. An ineffable, intangible spiritual luminosity shone over him, like an inextinguishable radiance. It was this that cast a spell upon all who drew near him. When he entered a room, all hearts were hushed.

When he opened his mouth to speak in his melodious, flute-like voice, his listeners were enthralled. And no wonder! For his words were not the words of an ordinary mortal. They were charged with the power of God's message – the message of Life, Light and Love!

It is my earnest hope that you, the reader, may also hear that beautiful message through the pages of this book!

J. P. Vaswani

Preface

In this book I present a few of my life's experiences. Life is full of experiences, many of which we tend to forget. I haven't even kept a diary to jot down the day-to-day happenings. But all my experiences have raised one eternal question. Who am I? Where is my home? In the ever-changing transient world there is nothing that I can call my own. Hence the question: Which is my native home?

Many towns and cities I have roamed, from Calcutta to Karachi, from Simla to Rameshwaram. Outside India too, I have been to many parts of the world. Many global events have happened during my lifetime. The two world wars which took place devastated several countries in the east and the west. The Political unrest and turmoil among the emerging nations of the Third World, makes it apparent, that war is not too far from us.

During my lifetime I have also witnessed the great revolution called Swaraj. But may I humbly submit that we have yet not achieved true freedom. There is an appalling poverty in our country, there is suffering in our villages, even our towns and cities lack the vibrancy, which would make India a world power.

I have witnessed drastic changes. I have seen economies crumble and nations fall. One of the dire consequences of Independence has been the partition of the country. This historic division of the sub-continent forced us to leave our native Sind. Alas! I am homeless and I shall die homeless. My Sind, my beloved Sind, a land of Saints and Sufis, of mystics and *fakirs*, of Shah and Sami, of Sadhu Hiranand and Sadhu Navalrai, has my soul. How often have I felt soulless and lonely, yet I cry out to the Lord '*Shukar, Shukar*'.

Our migration from Sind to India raised the same question again, Where do I belong? Which is my native place? Where is my real abode?

Once I was imprisoned. During my short stay in the jail, I learnt many lessons. There too I asked myself, 'Where is your home? Where do you belong?'

I am but a pilgrim on this earth. My whole life has been a quest. On one hand, I have been in quest of my Beloved. On the other hand my search has been for the land of the Spirit.

O! Swan, you wise bird tell me,
From which land have you descended? On which shore have you landed?

O! Swan bird of an alien land, tell me from where have you come? And how did you land on the shores of this country? It is true, I have immense love for my native land Sind. Time and again, have I pined for it. How often have I recalled the nostalgic words of that great Laureate Poet of Sind, Shah Abdul Latif.

Climbing the ramparts of the fort,
I gazed at Maleer,
Day in and day out,
I shed tears.

My heart cried,
My soul screamed,
But none came to enquire,
None came to console me.

I turned my face to my beloved land Sind, I got a glimpse of it. I wept tears for the glimpse of it. My heart cried, a soulful scream rented the air. But alas! None of my fellow beings heard me. And I said to myself, 'None of my neighbours have bothered to find out about my heart's cry?'

I still carry great affection for my native land Sind. Its memory is still alive. But I had to migrate. The first thing I did, after landing at Bombay was to find out about the condition of my Sindhi fellow beings. I searched for them in the refugee camps; some were staying in inhabitable places. How I wept for them!

Even now when I think of their condition, I feel deeply moved. Then comes the same questions: O! Traveller, Where is your real home? Which is our own country? The few experiences narrated in this book raise the same question again and again. Where is your home? Which is your country?

My dear brothers and sisters, my life has but one message: Your true home, your native land is in that country to which the saints have borne witness. It is that spiritual paradise and heavenly abode where there is no distance; no difference. Where Oneness holds a beacon of light to the universe.

O Swan Bird of Paradise,
Why have you landed
In this darkness?

My dear fellow beings I have this to say: Awake! Awake! Cultivate the soul and be blessed.

T.L. Vaswani

Translator's note

Sadhu Vaswani's life was a beautiful prayer. It was a river of spirituality. An Intellectual scholar, his thoughts flowed into endless poetry. It is difficult to translate such a great man's lyrical sacred works into prosaic of English language. Nevertheless, I have tried to balance the lyricism of his diction and the essence of his spiritual thought. It is likely that in keeping to his 'gentle words' I may have deviated from the rules of grammar, for which I seek your forgiveness.

I thank Dada J.P. Vaswani for giving me this rare opportunity of translating Gurudev Sadhu Vaswani's sacred words. It has indeed been an enriching and an exceedingly fulfilling experience for me.

Aruna Jethwani

Part-1

The Journey of Life Begins

I was born in Hyderabad Sind in a poor family. I grew up in austerity. My father Shri Lilaram, though according to official records a Zamindar, was in reality a man of meagre means. Sometimes he would take me along with him and buy me peanuts. One day he said, "Son I haven't eaten anything. I will satiate my hunger with a fistful of peanuts." My father's land was not too small. But its produce was meagre and provided bare subsistence for the family.

It is true that one of our relatives from the Vaswani family rose to be a famous lawyer. His name was Teckchand Audhavdas Vaswani. He was my father's cousin. He rose from dire poverty to become a wealthy man. When he passed away he left behind eight lakhs of rupees. He was one of the two well known people in Hyderabad Sind. He was also the President of Amil Panchayat for sometime. My father was a poor man. So my childhood was spent in utter poverty.

To tell you the truth I never did feel the pinch of poverty nor did I desire to amass wealth and be rich. One day, Mr. Teckchand called me and advised, "Be a lawyer and then join me in my profession." I said to him, "Sir, I am grateful to you for the offer, but my heart is elsewhere."

Right from my childhood saints and *darveshes* greatly fascinated me. Their spiritual teachings influenced my life. Even to this day I hum the song of Rohal *fakir*.

Alone you'll go from here,
Four things you need to heed,
One is to witness the truth
The second is to keep the Beloved near,
Third is to tread in fear,
The fourth is to abide by simplicity.
Then Oh! Rohal, you will,
Ever be near your Beloved's Durbar

The song conveys the essence of simplicity. Which means to be simple in your food habits and in your dress. Be simple in your day to day living, at your work place and in all your personal dealings.

During my childhood there were often occasions, when Hindus and Muslims clashed. Even then, I considered Muslims as my friends. My first school where my education was through Sindhi medium was on *'charhi'* (slope of hill). On one side of the *'charhi'* (slope) of the hill lived Negroes.

These Negroes were good in wrestling. Quite often I used to go to the play ground and watch the wrestlers in action. It used to delight me. In the wrestling both Hindus and Muslims participated which was indeed heartening.

My revered father did not know English, but he had mastery over Persian. I never learnt that language. I tried to learn Sanskrit for a while. Yet it was Persian, which enamoured me. Since my childhood I had great regard for some of the Persian poets. This love for poetry was the legacy of Rumi and Hafiz.

My dear father used to recite Rumi's Poetry and sing it with great gusto. I do recall, myself listening to Rumi's poetry with zest and enthusiasm. I could not understand the Persian words, but the lyrical language deeply touched my heart. As I grew up I began to enjoy Rumi's poetry translated into English. His poetry had magical effect on me. I began to realise that Rumi was not only a great poet, but also a great *Brahmagyani*, a knower of spiritual knowledge.

During the rule of *Mirs* in Sind, Rumi's lyrics used to be sung in the royal court and Rumi's poetry was taught in the schools. Rumi's voice carries one message:

'The flame of life is love.
The Ecstasy of life is love'.
In one place this great Sufi writes about God, which when translated reads:
Words cannot describe the radiance of Love,
Go within and behold the illumined One!

Rumi's love for the flute was wonderful. Its melodious notes would draw him into an ecstasy.

Flute is also a symbol of love. In one place Rumi writes, 'flute is the fire of love, which has burnt me alive'. Flute is love's wine, intoxicating. Through it I have seen the vision of my beloved. "O dear Man! If you want to know how true lovers shed tears of blood, then wake up and listen to the exotic music of the flute."

As a child studying in the nursery class, I was in the habit of smiling. Seeing my smile the teacher would be angry. In my mind I used to think, what kind of a teacher I have got, who says, don't smile, and don't laugh!

One day, the school got over early. I was happy returning home feeling elated. Thank God, I will be away from my teacher. I ran home as fast as I could. After meals I fell asleep. Hours passed. At last my father came and asked why I didn't go back to school. I said, "Baba I will not go. My teacher does not allow me even to smile." My father slapped me hard. But there was deeper meaning in that stern act. If my father would have not slapped me, I would not have gone back to the school and would not have sat for the exams. My father had my welfare at his heart. That slap was a blessing in disguise!

The slap was very painful. My cheeks went red. May I therefore say, to hurt someone is not a sin if it is meant to bring out the good in that person. Much depends on the 'intention' of the person. One's intentions should always be good.

My father's family used to celebrate Shivratri with great zeal. My father was a Shiva *Bhakta*. As a rule therefore, on a Shivratri night we remained awake to pray to Lord Shiva. On one such night my father came into the room and said, "I will take you to the Shiva temple." The temple had a facade of sculpted faces of 'Devil'. I sat inside the hall in a corner listening to the devotional songs.

After a while, it was announced that the *prasad* would be distributed. Thereafter the head priest of the temple came and distributed *'prasad'* with his own hands.

The Mahant was wearing simple clothes. I did not realise that he was the head priest. I asked those present there, "Who is this man?" and was told "he is the head priest". He offered me the *'prasad'*. What do I see? A piece of flesh in his hands. For sometime, I had abstained from flesh diet. When I realised that the Mahant was offering me that lump of flesh in form of *'prasad'*, my heart revolted. What should I do? For a few seconds I thought, it would be wrong to break my norms and eat that piece of flesh. Therefore with folded hands I pleaded with the priest, "Sir, Thank you very much. But please forgive me." The Mahant was stunned. He questioned me, "Why don't you accept it?"

I replied, "Sir, I will not be able to eat this flesh."

My beloved father was standing next to me. He went into a rage. He was furious because I had refused the sacred *'prasad'* offered by the head priest. My father slapped me hard, so hard that it is difficult for me to forget it even now. Then he dragged me out of the portal of the temple and said, "Don't sit here, you don't deserve to be here."

That was the first unsavoury experience of my life. I felt very hurt, because I was being forced into doing something which was against my wish.

On returning home my father again persuaded me to partake of that *prasad*. He also tried to make me drink alcohol. The Shiva devotees eat non-veg; they eat fish and drink alcohol on Shivratri day. But God gave me the courage to resist it. Bent on my knees I prayed to Almighty, to save me from the sin of eating animal flesh.

Once my father along with his friends was eating fish *'Palo'* on the banks of river Sindhu. Once again I was being forced into eating the flesh food. With folded hands

I told them to forgive me. "I will stand by my conviction," I said. I said it firmly.

Long ago, when I was a small child, my father took me to a Shivratri *Mela* (funfair) held on the banks of the Sindhu river. What do I see? I see crowds of people, colourful buntings, and other glittery. My father asked, "What do you want?" I replied, "Baba I want one thing."

"Which thing?"

I said, "Baba I want a balloon."

I saw the balloon and I fell for it. My beloved father bought it for me. I blew air into the balloon and it burst. But I learnt a lesson. The balloons will always burst. My father remarked rather wisely, "that the whole world is like a balloon, ephemeral and transitory. So, 'O! Child, link yourself with God." May we take this teaching to our heart? Everything in this world, all our possessions, and all our wealth is like that balloon which will burst. Even our existence is temporary. I remember one verse from the poetry (*Bani*) of Baba Farid, in which the fakir says:

> 'Farid will go,
> Dada will go,
> You too will go.
> And those who are left behind
> Will also go across to the shore.'

'Oh' dear man, your father has passed away; your Dadu has passed away. Be aware that you too will pass away; even your children will one day leave this world. The whole Universe is ephemeral. The whole world is like a balloon that will burst. Everything is transient. Only the light of the spirit shall remain forever.

This incident occurred when I was studying in the fourth standard. There was a death in the neighbourhood. Baba, my father was running fever, yet he insisted that he should attend the funeral. As a result, his fever rose high. My father was a *Tapasvi*, a worshiper of Kali Ma. He used to stand on one leg and worship Kali Ma for two hours everyday. He used to say that he had been blessed with the vision of Kali Ma. I nursed him during his illness. One day, after buying peanuts for one paisa, as I was returning home, I heard a voice say, 'Dear child today your father will pass away'. I threw the *'nakuls'* (sweet chickpeas) and came and sat by the side of my father. Since that day I have stopped eating *nakuls* (Sugar coated chickpeas).

During the days of his illness, I was the only one free at home. My mother used to be busy doing household chores. Through out the day, she slogged in the kitchen. I therefore took upon myself to go and sit by my father. I saw him suffer. I realised his days were numbered. My father liked the soft pressure of my hand and so he requested me to press his body to soothe the pain. As I pressed his body, all of a sudden, I saw him turn pale. I ran to call my mother who was working in the kitchen. She was tired and fagged out. We were poor and did not have any domestic help. From the look of my father, I felt that he was slipping away. I told my dear mother, "Ami, Baba is passing away." My mother came in to the room and sat for a few moments opposite my father. During those few moments, my father kept gazing at me with eyes full of love. Blessing me he said, "My dear son, God's Blessings are with you. You have served me well during my illness. Now it is time for me to go." After a few moments he breathed his last.

The Diwali following my father's death is vivid in my memory. It was a dark Diwali – filled with grief and gloom. It was dark because we were in mourning. My father's death in the house had plunged us into sorrow. The Diwali that I remember the most, was a dark and a painfully tragic one.

Who moulded my life? My mother's influence was greater than that of my father. I feel indebted to her. Even now at the very thought of her, I feel the surge of emotions overwhelming me. To Quote Shah Abdul Latif,

> My heart yearns for Mother,
> Every breath is Vibrant with her love,
> Mother, My beloved Mother,
> Every moment is alive with your memory.

Dear Mother, day in and day out I bow down to you to seek your Blessings. Mother, you have made my life so beautiful!

My mother moulded my life with the teachings of Guru Nanak Dev. I knew nothing about Guru Nanak. It is my beloved Mother who initiated me to the beautiful verses of *Gurbani* and *Sukhmani Sahib*. My mother did not receive formal education but she remembered *Gurbani* by heart. And at that tender age these verses made a deep impression on my heart.

I recall on an early morning one day, I entered the room. What do I see? A picture hanging on the wall and my mother standing besides it in a reverent mood. She is gazing at the photograph in the picture. Then she places her hands on the picture and then puts those blessed hands on my head. It is then that I ask her, "Mother whose picture is this?"

She replies, "Dear this is the sacred picture enshrined in my heart. It is the picture of Guru Nanak whom I worship."

I was sent to a Sindhi medium school. I remember hazily, I was studying in second standard. My dear mother touches the picture of Guru Nanak and blesses me saying, "My child we are poor, you are the only treasure I possess. You are my main strength. I hope that you will study and when you grow up, you will take care of me." Then she hastens to add, "But the great giver is the one Guru Nanak Dev." Again she bows down to the picture, moves her hand over it and transfers the blessings on to me.

My mother was the first person to draw me to the teachings of Guru Nanak Dev. She had wonderful love for the Guru. My father was a Shiva Bhakta and worshipper of Kali, but my mother was the devotee of Guru Nanak Dev. From my early childhood she had taught me to recite *Gurbani*. My mother insisted that I recite it every day before going to school. We had an early morning school and so my mother's instructions were, "First recite the *Gurbani* then have breakfast." To which I asked, "If the breakfast is not ready can I go to the school without it?" She answered, "Yes. It does not matter whether you have breakfast or not. What matters is the sacred recitation of the Guru's verses, from *Jap Sahib* or *Sukhmani Sahib*."

It often so happened that I had to go to the school without having breakfast. My mother used to give me one paisa – we were poor, so my pocket money was only a paisa per day, but that one paisa was sufficient to buy me *'Dal Puri'* in the school. A vendor used to come to the school compound and I used to buy *'Dal Puri'* from him. That one paisa coin contained her love and Blessings. Time and again my mother exhorted me, "Don't forget the Guru. In whatever conditions, under whatever circumstances he puts us, we should remember our Benefactor."

Since then the divine teachings of Guru Nanak Dev have made a deep impact on my heart. Time and again I have been reciting the divine name and savouring its nectar.

One day I ask my revered mother, "Mother! Why do you have such great devotion for Guru Nanak Dev? Why do you entreat me to recite his verses everyday?" My mother replied, "Guru Nanak Dev has taught me many things."

"What makes him a Guru?" to which my Mother replied, "Baba Nanak is called Guru because his teachings are full of wisdom." Then she recited:

Without a Guru there is no knowledge,
Without a Guru there is no meditation,
Without a Guru you can't learn *Atam Gyan*,
Without a Guru there is no discourse,
Without a Guru there is no Path.

It is through my mother that I learnt to bow down at the feet of Guru Nanak Dev. It is she who taught me to build my life, in the knowledge of the *Gurbani* and in the faith of the Guru.

I am passing on my mother's wise words to you. May you be so blessed by Guru Nanak, as to rebuild a new life, a blissful life; a life to be spent in the service of those in poverty, pain and suffering.

A few childhood memories are still fresh in my mind, even now at this stage of my life. Today's education is received through formal schooling and through printed books. But in my childhood, may be when I was six years old, I received education quietly at my mother's feet. In the night mother would cook a meal of *'Kichadi'*. As a child I used to wait impatiently for *'Kichadi'* to be cooked. I would urge my mother to serve the meal quickly as I would fall off to sleep. To keep me amused, my mother narrated anecdotes and episodes full of moral wisdom. In this way I learnt many valuable lessons of life and also acquired knowledge.

My mother lacked formal education; she did not know a word of Sindhi, for that matter even of Gurmukhi. The question of knowing English did not arise.

One night we were sitting in the courtyard. My mother gazed at the sky, and said, "Look at that star! How beautifully it shines!"

"Which is that star?"

"It is called Dhruv and the word Dhruv is loaded with meaning," she replied.

"Dear Mother, tell me the story of this beautiful Dhruv star."

My mother narrates the story in the following words:

Dhruv was a small child of a great King. Dhruv's mother came from a royal family and was a true devotee of the Lord. She did not relish the splendour of her palace, nor did she enjoy the luxuries of life. She meditated and prayed. This was the way she worshipped God. The king did not approve of it. He felt, that the queen should pay him more attention. She should join in enjoying the luxuries of life. Instead, the queen spent her time in silent prayer. Annoyed by her behaviour, the King felt, 'This woman is of no good for me.'

The King finds a new woman for himself. He marries her; that beautiful woman now becomes the queen and sits on the throne. The first wife, Dhruv's mother finds happiness at the lotus feet of the Lord.

At this time Dhruv is only five years old. One day Dhruv goes to the Palace '*Durbar*' and finds the new queen sitting on the throne along with his father. He runs towards her and climbs into her lap. The queen is mortified. She scolds Dhruv, "You are not my child, and you have no right to be in my lap." Saying so, she pushes him down. Feeling hurt, Dhruv rushes back to his mother, and weeps. "Mother tell me, how does one become a King? How does one claim the throne?" To which his mother replies, "Worship the Lord and the Lord bestows the bounty of throne."

At which Dhruv asks, "Mother show me the way to love the Lord. I too want to be worthy of a King's throne. This throne belongs to my father. I want a throne of my own."

The mother picks up Dhruv and puts him on her lap. She hugs him and wiping his tears says, "You are very young my child." But Dhruv insists. "Ami teach me to love the Lord."

His mother replies, "Not yet, you are still very young." To which Dhruv says, "Ami you must show me the way to the Lord. Which way and what path should I follow, to reach Him and love Him?"

Mother replies, "My dear child, go to the forest, go to *tapoban*, there is a large tree under which you should meditate. Then from your heart pour out love for the Lord. The Lord will surely come to you. The Lord goes to those who love him truly."

Dhruv goes to the forest, to the *Tapoban* and there he meditates on the Lord and pours out his love. Pleased at this, God goes to him and says, "Dear child, ask for a boon."

To which Dhruv says, "Tune the vocal chords of my throat, so that I may sing your name." God replies to him, "O' child Dhruv, I have tuned your vocal chords and the *chakra* of your throat is open. Now you will be able to sing melodious songs. In the soulful *Bhakti* you will experience me."

Dhruv is lost in the ecstasy of divine music. He sings the name Divine with deep devotion. He keeps singing the heavenly tunes. God is so pleased with his devotion, that he exalts him to a permanent place in the sky.

My mother pointing to the North Pole star says, "Look there, my child! How beautifully shines the throne of Dhruv!"

Even today, I reflect upon the beauty of the North Pole star. I marvel at my mother's words. "May you be so blessed as to sing God's name in devotion. May you ever shine like the star of Dhruv in the evening sky." Those words have deeply touched my heart.

As a small child, we lived in a lane which had a sweet (mithai) shop. Along it ran a drain. This shop was crowded by people. Many a times small coins would fall into the drain. Once a friend asked me, to comb the drain for coins. I cleared the drain. No sooner did I clear it, it was filled with slush again. Alas! We are like that drain. Our, minds are polluted. A brother once said to me, "My mind is vulnerable. When I sit at the *satsang* my mind gets purified. But the moment I step out, vicious thoughts assault me."

It is true, that the world around us influences us. This brother further said, "It is difficult for me to keep the mind pure. I clean the mind of impurities, but the dust and dirt of the world storms in, sullying it again."

"True enough my dear, it is difficult to keep the mind clean and pure. To purify the mind and keep it so, we need God's grace and the Blessings of the Holy ones."

As a child, I lived in a small humble mud house in a narrow lane. I was in the habit of waking up early in the morning, so that I could watch the sun rise. I would bow down to the rising sun and seek its blessings. I have immense faith in the *Shakti* of the sun. I would gaze at it till my eyes became wet. Then seeking its blessings, I would sit for some time in prayer and study scriptures. Our ancient Rishis believed that the *shakti* of the sun is able to hold the earth together, hence my prayer was, "O, Lord, may this power of sun hold me firm. May it cleanse my heart, and protect me from evil."

I also had the habit of going to the terrace in the night. There gazing at the moon, I would pour out my heart, "O' God! Make me calm and serene like the moon."

Even as a child I had immense faith in God. One day my mother told me that a dear one had lost his job and therefore was in dire straights. Her words stirred my heart. That night I fervently prayed to God to get him back his job. It may sound childish, but I did so, I prayed, 'My Lord, My God, My beloved! This dear one has lost his job and he is going through a tough time. He does not even have enough food to eat. Please God give him a job of Rs. 40." I was small and I thought that forty rupees is a very big amount. I therefore repeated the same prayer in the morning. For seven days and nights, I implored the Lord to get him a job with a salary of Rs. 40/-. On the eighth day my mother announced to the family that the relative had found employment for exactly that amount, adding, "I wonder, whose blessings have worked," Ah! How grateful was I to God! I have never spoken of my inner journey (hidden life) to anyone, but I can vouchsafe for one thing. Whenever I have prayed to God, and this I have done several times for the worldly good of others, he has answered them promptly.

In the Bhagavad Gita, Lord Krishna tells Arjun, "Anyone who comes to me in faith and humility, I shall answer his call. And he too shall cross over to the other shore."

When I was a little child, my mother one day dressed me in expensive new clothes. Filled with joy, I strutted around showing off my new clothes. A sister threw a bucket full of dirty water on me. The dirty water splashed on my clothes and stained them. I thought to myself: Thank Heavens! Here is a lesson for me to learn. Sin is like that dirty water. Our *Atman* is pure as crystal. But when it enters the gross physical body, evil desires of the world taint it. Sin is an evil which plagues the whole body.

I had great fascination for Nature's creation. Even now when I see a peasant ploughing the field, my heart jumps with delight. When I was in school, I used to sit in solitude, reflecting upon the placid waters of the lake near my house. Every year the lake would get dry, as the waters would run off to lower areas leaving wet patches of earth.

One day a thought came to me to sow some seeds in that wet patch of earth.

I sowed a few seeds. Every day I waited impatiently for seeds to sprout. After a few days, sprouts appeared; seeing this, my joy knew no bounds. Within a few days, the garlic pods grew. I was delighted and told myself that here is one more lesson to be learnt.

If you sow garlic, you will reap garlic. Then why not sow fruits like mangoes, grapes, custard apples, olives and musk melons?

I was enrolled in the newly opened School by Sadhu Hiranand. In the School, we were taught to recite *Sukhmani* and *Jap Sahib*. Right from the childhood, the Guru's teachings were infused in us. Sadhu Hiranand's brother was also a great *Bhakta* of the Lord. Few of us know of his spiritual altitude. He was the senior Deputy Collector of Hyderabad Sind. He held a position second only to Rishi Dayaram Gidumal. And yet he lived a highly noble life. He did his office work sincerely. After finishing the day's official duties, he would go to the Brahmo Mandir. The Brahmo Mandir had a temple with a vast open ground. It had a lovely garden, which Sadhu Navalrai watered and tended with his own hands.

Sadhu Navalrai had enshrined Guru Granth Sahib in the temple. It was here at Brahmo Mandir that Sadhu Navalrai spent most of his time. He used to get his meals from home and used to eat and sleep here. He lived a life of *'Vairagya',* detachment. Fully drenched in the devotion to Guru Nanak, he recited verses from Guru Granth Sahib all the time.

One day I happened to go to Brahmo Mandir. What did I see? Sadhu Navalrai is reading the Guru Granth Sahib with deep reverence. A small group of people was seated around him, listening to him in rapt attention. He was explaining the Guru's teachings to them. Thereafter he took his meals. Offering a small prayer, he retired to bed.

Sadhu Navalrai was indeed a grand noble soul. I found a reflection of his spirituality in his brother's school. At Hiranand's School we were taught *Gurbani* (Guru's words). We hardly comprehended its deep meaning, but whatever we understood gave us immense joy.

I have often contemplated on Sadhu Hiranand's life. I have reflected on his values and wisdom. I was curious to find out what Guru Nanak thought of him. So I used the "subtle" way of the "*Vachan*" to find out Guru's assessment of this noble and virtuous soul. I opened *Sukhmani Sahib* at random and the page had the following passage:

> The true Brahma *gyani* is,
> The one who is the true devotee of the Lord.
> The true Brahma *gyani* is,
> Who is pure and humble.
> The true Brahma *gyani* is,
> Who lives in Simplicity.

Sukhmani Sahib Eshtapadhi 8, Verse 4

This verse gives us the correct picture of Sadhu Hiranand. What a befitting description!

The main personality trait of Sadhu Hiranand was his utter humility. He spoke caringly and gently. Never did I see him get angry or speak harshly to his students.

In those days my eyes were giving me trouble. One day Sadhu Hiranand calls me and says, "O' dear, your eyes don't look well. Probably you are reading too much. Do not strain your eyes so much. Come with me and I will give you some medicine for your eyes." This God's good soul gives me the homeopathy medicine. Sadhu Hiranand used to practice homeopathy, an 'alternative medicine' but never accepted a pie in return from anyone. In fact, whenever he saw a sister or a brother wanting money, he would help them from his own pocket, saying, "Go and have some food." He was deeply concerned about the poor people. His life was rooted in simplicity and humility. He lived a life that was pure and noble indeed!

Initially the school had very few students. But within a few years, the strength of the school grew to be 500 students. Yet Sadhu Hiranand never did slap a student. Never did he speak harshly to anyone. He was referred to as 'Humble Hiranand'! He would go to the class in reverence and humility. One day he takes up a lesson from our textbook, titled 'fire'. He narrates amazing stories about 'fire'. What is fire? What is the relation between fire and electricity? Fire creates and fire destroys. With great enthusiasm he said, "Dear children, may every heart be lit by the fire of zest. May the flame of enthusiasm burn in your heart? May you be good citizens. May you be good patriots. May you become true devotees of the Lord."

One day a king visited Hyderabad (Sind). Probably he was the Raja of Kolhapur. The fame of Hiranand's School had reached him and he expressed the desire to visit the school.

Sadhu Hiranand met him and told him, "Welcome Sir, by all means you may visit my small humble school." He took the Raja around the school. Our teacher ordered 'stand up'. We did not know that the visitor was the king of a big state. He was a simple man. Later, we learned that he was a Royal King. As small children we were delighted to have a king as our visitor.

One afternoon Sadhu Hiranand meets me and says, "Dear one, some days ago your eyes had a problem and I gave you the medicine. I hope by the Divine Grace, you will need medicine no more." Since that day my eyes have not given me any problem. By his great blessings my eyes have been trouble free ever since.

It was a hot sizzling afternoon. Sadhu Hiranand said to me, "Today it is very hot and your eyes are weak. Do not go out in this heat" – "Sir, Where will I have lunch then?" I asked hesitantly. He replied, "Oh foolish boy, how could you ask such a silly question? You can have lunch with me." He sends his servant to his house with the instruction to bring lunch for two.

Sadhu Hiranand was the headmaster of the school, and I was his student. But he did not let that stand between us. After he fed me, he narrated many interesting anecdotes and as I listened to his words, my hunger for those 'goodie' stories increased. Then he asked me to go upstairs and rest for a while, as my eyes were weak. I took a short nap. After which he asked me to go and join the children playing on the ground. He blessed me with the words:

"Meet me after you finish playing with the children". Such was his humility. The words, 'the true knowledge seeker is a picture of humility' aptly applies to him.

Truly, Guru Nanak Dev sings sweetly, "I am humble; I am lowly." Same was the voice of Sadhu Hiranand.

I first read about Jesus Christ, when I was in Std. I. His stories amazed me. I read the Crucification of Christ, the nailing of his saintly body. Nailing of his hands and feet, his chest and all that he uttered was "Oh God forgive them for they know not what they are doing".

Further I read, that one day this great Son of God is thirsty and calls out, I am thirsty, and I am thirsty. Those words moved me and I wept. "Beloved, you are thirsty so am I. May you accept me at your lotus feet."

My Revered father came to know of my deep reverence and love for Jesus Christ. My father was a devotee and a *tapasvee*. For months together he would stand on one leg and recite verses from the scripture *Chandi Shastra*. He used to love and bless me. But when he came to know that in my heart I carried deep devotion for Christ, he felt unhappy. He feared that this love for Christ might convert me to Christianity. My father discussed this matter with me in an affectionate and candid manner. Time and again I reassured him, "Respected father, love does not compel to change one's religion; love strengthens the foundation of a pure and trustworthy life. Please bless me so, that I may be strong and be as solid as a rock. And that I should not move away from the Eternal Light which is dear to the truth seekers."

As I have grown in the years I have asked myself a question, who is our dear Jesus Christ? And what answer do I get? I get the answer in a dream. In the dream I see:

It is a beautiful garden blooming with flowers. I am there in the dream, in the dream I see Sri Isha (Jesus).

I gazed and gazed at his face and said, "My Beloved". In the dream I stood at his door and he asks, "Who is that one standing at the door?"

I reply, "I am your humble servant". He asks, "Why are you standing at the door?" I answer, "Sir, I have come to seek blessings at your lotus feet!" He asks, "What gives you the strength? Where is the proof of your sincerity?" I reply, "Lord, have a look at my bruised heart." He queries, "Who called you here?" I whisper,

"Lord your love and affection, your grace, your mercy and your immense and amazing love."

Sri Isha further says, "My dear child, calm your turbulent mind, tune your heart to me, so that I may unfold your heart and draw out melodies as a musician who tunes the strings, to draw out music from it.

In that dream I see Shri Isha- Jesus Christ- sit by my side on the grass. All round blossoms were blooming. Sri Isha spoke the words, which penetrated deep into my heart.

In the words of Jesus Christ —-
He who remains in equanimity is indeed happy.
He, who is not chained by the worldly wealth, is indeed free.
Those are the fortunate, very fortunate, who experience the pain and the agony.
And those who suffer in anguish ever smile and never complain.
Those are the very fortunate ones, for they are in the quest of Truth.
They alone in the world have found true peace: Compassionate in heart, Mercy in the soul for the birds and the beasts.

The beautiful words: Those who have pure love in their hearts, whose eyes anxiously search for the poor and the needy, and the broken ones, are fortunate indeed. Those who experience the pain of others are blessed indeed. Those whose hearts are pure; for them the veil of *maya* is lifted. They can behold the beauteous face of the beloved, through meditation.

The dream was over.

I opened my eyes, I was astonished – where is Jesus Christ? My lips were still moving with the words "My Beloved, Oh, My Beloved!" It was a mystical experience.

There was magic in Isha's words; I aspire to assimilate them and bear witness to his teachings.

While still at Sadhu Hiranand's School in Hyderabad, I was in the habit of keeping a small diary. I used to write my random thoughts, which turned out to be words of wisdom. Once I wrote my thoughts as follows:

"O Lord! May my heart be pure and soft like petals of a pink flower. May I bloom like a rose."

Silence is power. My first lesson was learnt in silence. My childhood was spent in a small mud house, which had one room down stairs and two rooms with a terrace on the first floor and very often after my meals, I would go upstairs and inside a small room, allotted to me by my father, I would sit in silence. I kept a stick in my room. From time to time I would make use of this stick. Do you know why?

I had read somewhere about a young saint who whipped himself at every evil thought that crossed his mind.

The whip would restore his equanimity. I also bought a sturdy stick from the bazaar. Whenever an evil thought or anger possessed me, I would hit myself with the stick. I was dead scared of the whip because it hurt me. I resolved silently. "O' God, if anger or an evil thought strikes me then I will strike myself with this stick."

I have also used another technique for keeping myself alert and mindful. Inside my garment I used to wear a garland of thorns. Anytime an evil desire disturbed me I would prick myself with those thorns. The blood would ooze out. It was a very painful exercise. Lord Krishna says, "Burn your desires before you come to me." I used the stick and the thorns to rid myself of the evil desires.

These simple methods of self-punishment had great effect on my life. In silence I would whip myself with thorns. My family, mother, father and uncle were unaware of the torture I inflicted on myself. In silence I learnt the meaning of life.

May I never forget that lesson ever! Although I have advanced in years, I am in the 83rd year of my life; I am yet not free of demonic thoughts. Nevertheless, I am seized by an intense desire to make my life pure, gentle and godly.

May I never forget this one lesson even now at this advanced age? I always had a deep yearning to be at the Lotus feet of the Lord. I keep reciting the prayer, which is dear to all saints:

"This heart is sad and gloomy.
May everyday I receive your Benign Mercy, my Lord.
In longing for you may I become cheerful?"

May, my beloved Lord keep me at His lotus feet. May He in His great mercy ferry me across to the Native shore.

Many years ago, plague struck Hyderabad city. People were dying. People were leaving their homes. One of my teachers called me aside and said, "I feel like eating ice, can you get me some ice?" He wanted to have ice from the famous shop, which was close to my house. My neighbourhood was called 'chowk'. The teacher said, "There is that sweet meat shop in 'chowk', go there and buy some ice for me."

A teacher's request was an order for me. I was afraid; the plague was rampant, and people were dying, but I had to obey the orders of my teacher. I plucked up enough courage to go out to 'chowk' and buy the ice from that particular sweetmeat shop. My hands were trembling and I kept muttering to myself 'the sooner I go away from this filthy place the better; because the plague may strike any time.' I was hounded by the thought of plague.

Do you know, I was tempted to buy the same ice for myself? The teacher had given me 4 annas to buy the ice for him. Now, I wanted to buy the ice for 4 annas for myself. I rebuked myself, "Oh fool. The monster of plague is looming large over the city." On the other hand the temptation to buy the ice grips me tight. Hurriedly I bought the ice and ran fast to give it to the teacher. Such is the nature of desire. It is a double-edged sword, it hurts you both ways. True '*Vairag*' lies in the renunciation of desire.

I was still in school when I went to live in a small village of Sind. In that village, a Sindhi officer allowed me to stay in his house. In the morning I witnessed a moving scene. This official was sitting in his courtyard and many poor peasants, some Muslim farmers; a few traders were gathered around him. They requested the official to write out applications for them. They wanted to file a complaint against the authorities. The *Amaldar* demands fees for writing out the applications." Pay me a rupee each then alone will I write an application for you."

Tears filled my eyes. This was a revelation to me. The Government officials plucking money out of the poor and miserable village folks. Compulsion of this kind is denial of kindness. Sant Tulsidas says: *'Daya Dharma ka mool hai.'*

Compassion is the root of religion. An authority has power, which is to be used for the betterment of people. But alas! It is often abused. And the weak and the lowly, who do not have money even to feed themselves, are milched dry. These poor people narrate their sad plight to *'Amaldar'*; but he insists that, each one should pay him 4 annas. The poor folks paid 4 annas each but their eyes were misty with unshed tears. The *'Amaldar'* compelled them to pay and felt happy over it. This is called the power of Authority. But the true *Shakti* lies in Compassion, which forms the essence of all religions.

Hyderabad Sind has a beautiful temple, the Brahmo Samaj. It was built by Sadhu Navalrai. The temple exudes peace and harmony. Often I would go there and sit in silence. I had an urge to spend more of my time in the serenity of its silence. At that time I had no desire to study further. My aim was to be a matriculate. A matriculate earned a salary of Rs.30/- and I thought: I would keep Rs.15/- for my basic needs and give Rs.15/- to my mother to run the house. This thought was fixed in my mind. Sitting in silence in the peaceful precincts of the temple, I contemplated on moulding my life. I had great fascination for the *Fakirs*. I longed for their company. I hungered for the spiritual wisdom of saints and sages.

One day my revered mother asked me, "what do you wish to become? What is your aim in life?"

I replied, "Ami, in my heart is the desire to become a *fakir*. I have fallen in love with the enlightened souls. I aspire to live as a *fakir* among *fakirs*."

My mother's eyes filled with tears. She said, "My dear child, please do not do so. If you will, then I would be deeply hurt. As long as I am alive, do not abandon the world. Once I cross over to the other shore, you may by all means renounce this world, and become a *Fakir*."

I promised her that I would abide by her word. It is under such circumstances, that I decided to join the college and study further. My aim was to land up a good job and earn fair amount of money for my mother. May be after she was gone, I would be free. I would become a *Fakir*. It happened as I had wished. One night my beloved mother passed away in Karachi. The very next day I sent in my resignation letter to the college.

All along, an urge to seek the company of saints and sages has remained with me.

My thirst for the spiritual knowledge has grown by leaps and bounds. For my heart belongs to the Lord (*Lahuti*) the Beloved, the Invisible and the Infinite.

My brush with Upanishads began while I was in the matriculation class. I learnt the first few lessons of this great Scripture at the feet of a Bengali Brahma Gyani. He was a renowned Sanskrit Scholar. One day he made me sit by his side. "Let me enlighten you about the wisdom of Upanishads," he said. Then he picked up a small book and opening it, he explained the meaning of a verse. In that paragraph, the *rishi* gives the message, that *whatever is, is the Vesture of Lord*. Everything in the world, every living being, and every thing that breathes is an image of God. Every man, every girl, every child, is Divine. Only if we would understand this, our hearts would be pure and loving. When one understands the meaning of it, one grows in the reverence for all life.

Further the *Rishi* exhorts us: (*Taiyan Tayakatyan Bhanjita*) all that is there should be renounced to attain happiness. Whatever you want to enjoy: high position; great possessions, then you must learn to renounce it. Cast away all your attachments. Oh dear one, be free of the worldly possessions. He who is detached from the material wealth is indeed wealthy, for he can really experience the joy of it. It is a mistake to think that by possessing materialistic things, we will gain happiness. The *Rishi* states the principle of Happiness as: True happiness stems from the detachment. Do not nurse mundane thoughts of possessing material things. Oh dear one, do not covet temporal worldly possessions. Because the true happiness arises out of *Tyag*.

Upanishads intoxicated and excited me. Even now I feel that way and get joy out of its teachings. I began to learn and to recite the verses of Upanishads. And gradually the yearning to give up all that is materialistic grew in me. I must confess it was not an easy task. The philosophy of detachment made a deep impression on my life. I have endeavoured to put it into practice. That is to give up all the worldly pleasures and possessions, to give up the comforts and luxuries of life, and to give up excitement and entertainment of social gatherings. If I were to be asked," What is your aspiration in life?" I would answer, "By renouncing the worldly comforts, may I find true happiness. The true bliss, the bliss of the native shore."

The first time I went to Bombay, I was to appear for the First year Arts examination. I carried a deep desire to have a glimpse of Lokmanya Tilak. Unfortunately I learnt that Lokmanya was in the jail. I went to the jail to meet him. I was questioned on the purpose of meeting him.

The authorities dismissed me by saying, "You are a college student. What business do you have to meet him?" I was not granted the permission to see him. That wish remained unfulfilled. I returned disappointed, and dejected. Yet his powerful words "Swaraj is my birth right" rattled in my mind. I have not been able to forget them. Those words were a '*Mantra*' for me.

Hyderabad Sind has a library called "native free library", which was a storehouse of books and magazines. It was the meeting ground of intellectuals who would exchange notes and discuss many things. We did so in the open air. We put out two chairs; one for a gracious lady by the name of Basanti Devi, often referred to as Yogini, a woman who was an epitome of virtues. The other chair was for the President of the meeting Mr. Teckchand. He too was a man of grace, nobility. Mr. Teckchand was a great orator and a learned man. A lawyer by profession, he had made a fortune for himself. He was my dear father's cousin. These two persons had made a mark in the Presidency of Bombay. One was Chandurwarkar, a high court judge and a great orator and the other was Mr. Teckchand my father's cousin.

The partition of the country pushed me out of my native home. I came to Poona out of compulsion, rather than out of choice. Long before this I had visited Bombay, on my own and it was a joyful experience. I was fortunate enough to hear the great orator Justice Chandurwarkar. Later this great-learned man came to Sind to preside over a conference. It was his greatness that when he came to Karachi, he enquired about me. It became my duty to call on him. However I was late in reaching him. Nevertheless, I heard him; his English as well as oratory, both were very good.

Annie Besant Devi- Besanti Devi- was also a great orator. Her speech drew people to her like a magnet.

She would hold the audience spell bound by the power of her speech. I heard Annie Besant speak in Hyderabad Sind. What was the essence of her lecture? Hindu religion is the ancient religion of *Rishis* and saints. Glorify it.

Those were the times when agnosticism reigned high in Sind. Young boys and girls openly denied the existence of God; others opted for conversion to Christianity or Islam. Social thinkers were aghast at this turn of happenings. A few intelligent boys proclaimed that they would be Muslims; a few others said they would become Christians. Yet others said, "We are Agnostic!" Such was the religious climate prevalent in Hyderabad Sind at that time.

Hyderabad Sind had the distinction of having an intellectual devotee of the Lord: Rishi Dayaram Gidumal. As a District Judge he was highly respected by the people. He became concerned about this new trend of thought. He decided to do something about it. He invited Annie Besant to Sind to address the youth in English and convince them about the richness of Hindu Culture. He wrote to her: "Kindly come to Hyderabad Sind and deliver a few lectures for our youth." Annie Besant replied, "I will come to Sind only for seven days. Three days I will spend in Hyderabad and three to four days in Karachi."

Large crowds of people gathered to listen to her. I too attended her lectures and was impressed by her oratory. After listening to her, I went home and sat in a solitary corner. I began to plead with God, "O' God you have bestowed on Annie Besant the gift of oratory. When will you bless me with such a gift?"

I was wonder struck by her eloquence, by her emotion filled voice which has left an indelible mark on my heart.

One day my college friends asked me to go out with them. Normally I went for my walks all alone. That day I was sporting enough to agree to their request.

These college friends took me for a ride. As we walked I noticed that they were signaling to each other and exchanging meaningful glances. I was unable to understand their peculiar behavior. It was around sunset time. The night darkness spread its wings and descended on us as a cloud. Yet we continued to walk, till we came to a small narrow lane. My friends made me stand there and laughed. In a moment they disappeared, saying they would be back soon. The place was new to me. It looked strange and weird. I found myself standing in front of a door of a house. A beautiful girl made her appearance at the door. I was impatiently waiting for my friends to return. I did not know where I was or else I would have returned home by myself. This beautiful girl gazed at me and beckoned me to come inside. I was hesitant.

At last she said, "Come inside so that we can have a soulful chat."

I did not know who she was. Realisation dawned on me rather late. I prayed to God, "Oh God! Great is your mercy. You have well protected me. You have saved the honour of an innocent one."

The beautiful girl gestured to me again. I understood the meaning. Collecting all my wits I said to her, "Sister, *Ram Simar, Ram Simar Yehi tero Karj hai*. Recite the name of the Lord for that is your destiny."

True this courtesan was a good singer: her voice was sweet, but she had walked the way of sin. She tried to snare me into temptation. I made a hasty retreat. At that moment I reflected within. I walked back home alone. On the way I prayed, "Thank you God! For protecting me from the sin of evil." As I walked, I repeated "Thank you God! Thank you God!" Again and again I uttered the words. Recite the name of the Lord. That is your goal.

The summer nights in Sind were very warm and our mud house was like a hot furnace. Therefore I preferred to sleep out in the open on the terrace. Lying under the canopy of the sky, I would gaze at the twinkling stars and sometimes watch the moon rise above the star of Venus in the Milky Way. I was in love with the star spangled sky and marveled at the moon in its various moods. Later at college I pursued my higher education, and I became acquainted with Astrophysics. I would gaze at the infinite space in wonder. And ask myself who are you?

A mound of mud? Though I was only a fistful of dust, God had been very kind to me. God had put me on a pedestal. I was blessed with the company of the affluent, the royal kings and queens, and the erudite scholars.

But in my heart, I carried the lesson, 'you are a mound of mud.'

Right from my childhood, a question had been troubling me. This question became an obsession. When I grew up, the question which still continued to trouble me, was: Sai, what is the truth? Sai reveal the truth. The question kept pestering me again and again. I asked many seekers: What is the Truth? What is the ultimate reality?

I am a pilgrim on the road of life. I am a *yatri*. I am in quest of Truth. I am puzzled: everything is an enigma to me. Is there anyone, any devotee of Lord, who will unfold the mystery of this life? Who will show me the luminous face of the Infinite? Even as a college student my mind refused to concentrate on studies. My heart was averse to the mundane affairs of life. It was a task to bring myself to be in this world of *'Maya'*. For deep within me was a yearning, to go to the root of the ultimate reality.

I lived in the world but my heart was not in it. Every day after returning from college, I would seek solitude in a garden and ponder over the same question: what is the ultimate reality? What is the mystery behind this creation?

When I completed my college education, my mother asked me a question, which disturbed me greatly. "It is high time you get married," she said. I was in a dilemma. Sitting in the solitude of the garden, I prayed repeatedly. Oh! God give me the strength to be away from marriage, so that I must spend my whole life in your service. However, on returning home, my mother would again pester me to get married. In the beginning I was firm and harsh and bluntly said no to marriage. Soon I realised it caused a storm at home. Thereafter I remained silent. Nevertheless, I was restless and confused. I prayed to God to send me away to another place, to another destination. For some time I had nurtured a desire to leave my home and to seek my livelihood elsewhere. For all along I was being chased with the proposals of girls, people tried to rope me in saying, "that girl is beautiful; that girl is pretty; that girl is virtuous, that girl is from a prestigious family." It pained my heart. I prayed to be spared from marriage. "Let me serve you, Oh, Lord!"

One day a relative of ours dropped in. He was an elderly man with worldly wisdom. At one time, he occupied a high position in the state of Bhavilpur, and was held in high esteem by the family. He asked my mother: "Where is your son who refuses to get married; bring him to me."

I was presented to this elderly man. In reverence I bowed down to touch his feet. He put me off by saying,

"Are you aware that the neighbourhood is on fire?" I asked, "Sir, what 'Fire'?" He replied, "The entire neighbourhood is against you. They are annoyed by your refusal to marry. I have come to plead with you and to drive some sense into your head."

Once again in reverence I bow down to him and hesitantly said, "What is the truth? What is the ultimate reality?" This relative of mine was astonished beyond words. What kind of boy is he?

There was a prolonged silence. At last I plucked up enough courage to repeat my query. "Sir, tell me the Truth. Tell me, what is the ultimate reality?" This relative was greatly agitated. He questioned my mother, "You told me that your son was educated but what he speaks makes no sense to me." On repeating the same question to him, the relative commented, "He is mad. He is a lunatic." That did not deter me from repeating the same Question. "What is the ultimate reality? What is the truth? Disgusted, this relative gave up on me; calling me names and demeaning me as an absolute lunatic. Thoroughly puzzled, he left the house in a huff.

How true it is! If you want to be free from the monstrosity of this world, then you have to be mad enough to match it. You have to do what the saints have said, *"follow the unbeaten path."* There is no other way. Instantly after the relative left, I ran up to the attic room, and sat in silence. I wept; I implored the Lord, "Please save me from the fetters of marriage."

As the quest for the truth grew, I yearned to run away from Hyderabad Sind. The matchmakers like Kishoo's mother brought proposals and created hassles at home.

This unsettled me. I got very confused. My thirst for the Ultimate Truth increased and I kept praying, "O, Omnipresent God, guard the honour of this servant of yours."

Sitting in solitude, I have reflected on this over and over again. A thought came to my mind which I have written down as:

> *"Not for a moment O Nuri enter the slushy waters of the world."*
> This world is a vast sea. It is an ocean; so do not step into it even for a moment lest you may be swept away by the tide.
> The night is dark! What will you search in the darkness?

O, dear me! The night is pitch dark, and the world is a whirlpool. Why do you want to enter into the whirlpool and be dragged into its depths? It is then, that I ask of the Omnipresent Divine Consciousness, to reveal to me the purpose of my life; the goal I should pursue. That Divine Consciousness, the Omnipresent Beloved, God the Sustainer of this Universe flashes an answer to me: "Dear, the goal of your life is to be a friend, to be a servant, to be a helper and protector of the poor, the needy and those in pain and suffering. Go and serve them and you will find the Lord."

There is no gain without pain. I learn this, while still studying for my B.A. Examinations. I had a desire to become a fellow of the college. A fellow received a stipend of Rs.50/- and at the same time was allowed to keep the terms for M.A. I wanted to study hard and get a rank with the first three positions, so as that I could be eligible for the post of fellowship. I worked very hard. On my vacations when I went to Hyderabad, I used to study until late in the night. I had a table and a chair kept on the terrace of the house. In those days, we did not have electricity. My mother would light a lantern for me. I would begin my studies at 9 o'clock after taking my meals. I would continue studying well beyond midnight. My mother encouraged me to do so and often brought me a cup of tea to keep me awake. I was permitted to study up to 2 o'clock in the morning. I used to get tired and fagged out. Nevertheless I goaded myself to study in order to live up to my mother's expectations.

My B.A. examination over, I anxiously waited for the results to be declared. On the day of the result, I locked myself up in the room. I began to plead with the Lord, Please don't let me down. Do make me pass the B.A. examination. After a while there was a knock on the door. A telegram was delivered. I was seized with fear, so much so that I refused to sign the telegram receipt. I grabbed the telegram, closed the door and with a palpitating heart, I opened it. Rupchand Balaram, who later became the judicial magistrate of Sind, sent the telegram. He was two years my senior. He happened to be in Bombay. He was so thrilled by my success that he immediately wired me the message: You have stood first in English in the University of Bombay. You have won the Ellis Scholarship.

I was not even aware of Ellis Scholarship, so I checked with the University Calendar. I was overwhelmed to see my results. After two days, I received a letter from the Principal of the College, stating that a student of his college had stood first at the B.A. examination and that should be me. I was awarded books and Rs.100/- for this achievement.

The credit for the academic honour received by me goes to my mother. I was appointed 'Dakshina Fellow' in Karachi College. I passed M.A. exam in 1902. My mother urged me that I should take up Law. "Your uncle is a lawyer and see how much he earns! You too become a lawyer and earn great wealth for me." I assured her that I would earn enough money for her. I took up teaching in Hiranand Academy. I had hardly worked for a few months when I received a telegram inviting me to be a professor in the Calcutta College. I sought my mother's permission. Her reaction was negative. "How will you go so far to Calcutta?" She cried. I went up to the terrace for solace and guidance; I prayed fervently. My mother ultimately granted me the permission. I sent her my first salary and it pleased her immensely.

In Calcutta - 9, Chidamodi Lane

At the feet of the Master

As said earlier, I received a telegram from one of the prestigious colleges of Calcutta, asking me to join them as a Professor of History and Philosophy. They requested for my consent by telegram. The telegram came as a storm in a teacup. How will you go so far? This was the question put to me, by my near and dear ones. True; Calcutta was even further than Delhi. I discussed the matter with a few elders in the family. They expressed their concern and said, "You are still very young to go so far away from home. Are you crazy?" But I longed to be away from home. I sent a telegram to the Principal of the college, thanking him for the offer and informing him of my consent to join the college.

In Calcutta, I began my career as an ordinary Professor in Metropolitan College [Vidya Sagar College]. This stint in college was merely to earn a livelihood. Within me was a deep spiritual yearning. I was clear in my mind that I was here only as a pilgrim in quest of the Infinite.

I was often called a professor, but I kept reminding myself, "I am a pilgrim. I am in quest."

Within me was the cry, "O' God, you have given me refuge in your fold; now show me the path to *Dargha*, or a shrine, where I may find thee. Where is that *Dargha*? Where is that shrine? It is not in the house of bricks; it is not a place of marble mausoleum. *Dargha* is the holy abode of an evolved soul.

With this kind of spiritual urge nudging me, I sought the paths leading to that *Dargha*.

By that time, Shri Ramakrishna had left his physical body. Another holy man Shri Keshab Chandra Sen was also not in this world. Yet, I was in search of a living guru.

Swami Ramkrishna has said, "Gold is dust and dust is gold."

Until and unless the gold and dust are equal in the eyes of man, he cannot follow the sacred path of spirituality.

Shri Keshab Chandra Sen taught his disciples that God resided in each one of us. He further taught that in all the religions, in all the nations, in all the countries, He alone resides and draws everyone to Himself. By the time I reached Calcutta, both these great souls had left their physical bodies.

The third great man was Swami Vivekananda. He too passed away before I could reach Calcutta. Swami Vivekanand had gone to America to spread the message of ancient Rishi culture of the East. On his return he gave the clarion call to the people of India for the same.

"Awake, Arise! O' People of *Bharat*. Slumber not! The West is eager to learn the teachings of the East.

Awake! Arise! Imbibe the spirit and the values of Ancient India."

Alas! Vivekanand was no more. He had passed away at a very young age.

I asked myself the question, where shall I seek the truth?

Overwhelmed by that thought I went to see a holy place. For me it turned out to be a true pilgrimage. That holy place was Dakshineshwar temple. Dakshineshwar Kali Temple is near Calcutta. I visited it. Why? Because it is built in the memory of the great saint Shri Ramakrishna Paramhansa. How I wish I could tell you some of the amazing stories of this great Saint. I feel like unfolding my heart to pour out inspiring anecdotes from the life of this truly great one.

One day I visit his living quarters in the beautiful garden of Dakshineshwar. Amid the well-laid out garden is a temple and near the temple is a small room. It is here that this saint lived. This room is sacred. May its sacredness remain here eternally.

One of the residents took me around to see the place. The Saint's room had a few relics and memorabilia.

I consider myself fortunate to have seen them. Few relics, insignificant, but my heart thumped with delight seeing them. Swami Ramakrishna Paramhansa's room was kept as it was. In the room an earthen lamp burns, day and night.

And do you know where this lamp was? It was placed in front of the picture, which was very dear to Shri Ramakrishna Paramhansa. That picture was of Jesus

Christ. Shri Ramakrishna Paramahansa was very fond of Jesus and he used to light a lamp in front of his picture everyday. Even after he had passed away, the earthen lamp was kept burning before the picture of Jesus Christ.

I bowed down before that picture and also that of Sri Ramakrishna Paramahansa. My eyes brimmed with tears. It is amazing how Jesus Christ has penetrated into my heart. Sri Ramakrishna Paramahansa did not consider Sri Isha as an outsider. He always referred to him as my dear or my beloved.

Calcutta is a city where I am in quest of solace: In search of a shrine of blessings. I visit many holy places. One day I am drawn to a small house in a lane. I go up the stairs, and find there are many rooms, but in one room a group of people are seated. They appear to be educated. A few among them speak only Bengali. To my great astonishment I find that some of them were college students. They were engrossed in chanting.

Hari Bol! Hari Bol! Hari Hari Hari Hari Bol.

This group of devotees had immense yearning for the Lord. Sitting amidst this gathering was the one who drew my attention.

I gazed at him again and again. He too, looked into my eyes. His enchanting smile captured my heart. I was pulled into his loving fold.

Locked in his gaze, I told myself: the eyes of this dear one are luminous radiating light. I had seen many people but the eyes of this man are different. They are breathtakingly beautiful: gentle and pure. Surely here is a man of God.

I say to myself, "O my beloved, you are the King of many hearts. You are also the King of my heart."

What an amazing personality! The man is simple, humble, feigning to be ignorant. We, the ordinary people love to demonstrate, but the true devotee of the Lord, keeps himself hidden.

He was amazing; his brilliant eyes glowed. By looking into his eyes I found solace. But I restrained myself. I should wait for a while, I cautioned myself. I should test him, before I take a step further. Even St. Mira sings:

'I went in search of Shyam and I found him, but not before I was convinced.'

St. Mira opines: I accepted Shyam after much deliberation and examination.

Even when we buy a small trinket in the market, we examine it carefully. I cajoled myself, "wait for some time. Find out more about him and then decide to take him as a Guru."

Sitting at his lotus feet, I try to find out more about him. Day by day, I felt impressed by this small group of people chanting, *Hari Bol, Hari Bol*. What a wonderful group they made! Everyday they chanted the name of the Lord. Compared to them I was a dry dead leaf. Some people used to call me Professor and invite me to various functions to give lectures. I felt proud and honoured to be given such opportunities. I used to savour the praises showered on me at such lectures, which were often presided over by renowned scholars. I lived my life in two halves. On one hand I was pulled by spirituality, on the other hand the adulation poured on me flattered my ego. I was foolish. Alas! I felt morose and sad; why do I not follow the path, which this man of God is showing to his devotees? All the time they are chanting *Hari Bol! Hari Bol!*

Hari Hari Hari Bol. Engulfed by these thoughts, I remember having assured myself with the words, "do nothing that brings you fame". But I failed to implement this in real life. The small voice within rapped me, "Act, but do not be afraid of criticism. Run not after the fame and glory of this world."

While I was in Calcutta, an intense yearning to find a man of God, who would show me the spiritual path, seized me. By the grace of God, I did find such a man. His name was Naluda. What does Naluda mean? In Bengali Dada is called 'Da' and his name was 'Nalu'. I used to call him 'Gurudev'.

"Do not call me Guru," he said. But deep within my heart, I was sure he was my Guru. He affirmed, "I am not a Guru, I am Dada: an elder brother. Do you know the true meaning of Dada? Dada is one who gives; the one who always gives."

In today's world, there are Gurus who take from their disciples, but Naluda was a true Guru, who did not ask for anything, but shared what he had. "Ask for the spiritual wealth, for that's what I have. I am your Dada, the giver." What beautiful words. Naluda's eyes glowed with affection. Never did he consider himself above us.

In fact he thought of himself as a servant of all.

One day he calls me and says, "my dear, come to me and I shall give you 'Naam'." I was excited. What

'Naam' will he give me? I wondered.

He, my Guru Naluda came from a reputed family of Bengal. He had his education at the Manchester College in U.K. He was a great Sanskrit scholar and he had done extremely well in his studies abroad. But he was as humble as a bee. After doing his work, he would meet us in his small room in that small house located in the lane by name of Chidamodi.

Such a man wanted to have me as his disciple! I was thrilled and I bowed down at his lotus feet. He smiled. His smile was magical. His smile was as fragrant as 'musk' of deer.

What 'Naam' will he give me? I wondered.

"From today onwards I shall call you *Boka*," he says gently.

I am surprised. My beloved Dada has an enigmatic smile on his face.

I too smile and smilingly ask: "Sai', pray tell me the meaning of 'Boka'."

"Boka means a fool," he smiles back. Then he adds, "You are a fool, you cannot follow the spiritual path unless you are convinced that you know nothing and that you are as ignorant as a fool." Since then the word Boka has teased me. True enough I was a fool. How can one acquire knowledge without realising the limitations of the 'self'? Since that day, our bonds grew stronger.

One day he comes over to my room and says, "Boka, tomorrow you should come with me, to visit such and such place." This made me feel very happy. After lecturing at the college, I would go and sit in silence at my Guru's feet. The students in the college reverently called me 'Professor'. But this 'Professor' was Boka at the feet of his Master.

The master had shown great mercy in calling me 'Boka'. Everyday I would sit at his feet and gaze into his loving eyes.

"The eyes of my beloved are luminous with Love. O' the great giver! You are the King of many hearts."

Henceforth I began to spend more time at his holy feet. In him I found the true marks of a spiritual man. A spiritual man has nine qualities. Those all nine qualities of spirituality were present in him. My faith in him deepened. I made him my guru.

I would like to enumerate all those nine qualities in order to reveal the great spirituality of my Guru Naluda. I have penned these nine qualities in the form of a lyric.

> Nine marks of a holy man, may you witness;
> The first is, gentle eyes, glowing with light.

The first mark of a spiritual man are his eyes which are radiant with love.

My Guru Naluda's life was pure: his disposition gentle. He was '*BAL Brahamacharya*'. His eyes brimmed with love Divine.

> The second mark of a holy man: He lives in utter humility. He bows in reverence to one and all.

The second mark of a spiritual man is his humility.

My Guru Naluda was humble. This humility was seen in his day-to-day life.

To illustrate this let me take you to our Ashram in that small lane in Calcutta.

Our Ashram had a cook who used to make food for the inmates. My Guru Naluda never treated him as a servant. He showed him great affection and treated him with utmost humility. Instead of calling him to do the various chores, he himself would go to him and request him in a humble way, to do a particular task. He addressed him endearingly as "my dear one". One day, pointing to me, he asked him, "Do you know who our guest is this evening?" Then he himself added, "Our guest has come from far off Sind. So kindly put *ghee* in the rice while cooking it." In Bengal, rice is cooked without *ghee*. This concern for my food was indeed touching. He took great pains to see that I was comfortable.

The third mark of a saint is: His life of simplicity.

The third mark of a spiritual man is his simplicity.

My Guru Naluda had a large family. He belonged to a well known family of Bengal. His uncle Keshab Chandrasen was a well-known social and religious thinker. Yet my Gurudev wore simple ethnic clothes, dhoti and kurta. Although he had received his education abroad - in Manchester, he did not sport western attire. Truly, he was an epitome of simplicity and austerity.

The fourth mark of a saint is:
He speaks less; he is a man of silence.

The fourth mark of a spiritual man is that he is a man of silence.

My Guru Naluda spoke few words. Most of his time he spent alone in silence. But his silence was eloquent It was vibrant with spirituality.

The fifth mark of a saint is his forbearance:
He bears suffering with a smile.

The fifth mark of a spiritual man is that he suffers physical pain, quietly and silently.

My Guru Naluda suffered from acute constipation. This often gave him discomfort. He would return from the washroom without finishing the job. At that time he would move his hands on the stomach – a sight that sent us into peels of laughter. He bore this physical discomfort quietly and with patience.

Sixth mark of a holy man is:
He is empty of desires and possessions.

The sixth mark of a spiritual man is that he has renounced all desires.

My Guru Naluda truly had renounced the world. Whatever wealth and property my Guru Naluda had inherited, he distributed among his family members, without keeping anything for himself.

Seventh sign of a man of God:
He remains awake during the night,
Communing with Him through Nama kirtan.

The seventh mark of a spiritual man is his night vigil.

My Guru Naluda used to be awake all **night. In that wakeful state he prayed to God, rejoicing in his name.**

Eighth mark: He sees God's image in the suffering humanity.

The eighth mark of a spiritual man is his kindness for suffering souls.

My Guru Naluda used to bow down to the poor and the needy. When asked, why he did so, he replied: "These poor down-trodden people are the pictures of God." Just imagine the unkind treatment we mete out to the poor and the needy, unaware of the fact that these too are broken images of God. They should be shown utmost kindness.

The ninth mark of a man of God is: His face glows while he is asleep, his breath exudes the name of the Lord.

The ninth mark of a spiritual man is the radiance on his face while he is asleep.

My Guru Naluda had a beautiful glow on his face while he was sleeping. To ascertain this we used to sneak into Guru Naluda's quarters, while he was fast asleep. His door would be kept ajar. We would gingerly open the door and then tip toe inside to have a glimpse of the radiance on his face. His every breath exuded the perfume of 'Naam'.

The glow on his face was dazzling. As if an inner light had shot through the gross physical to spread the divinity around. What do saints experience in such a state of wakeful sleep? Whom do they meet? What light do they see? Perhaps they meet the angels. This beloved one's sleep was a silent prayer: worship unto the Lord. He had the fragrance born of chanting the name of the Lord.

I try to be in Guru Naluda's company as much as possible. One day I ask him: Kindly tell me what have I to do? He who had nick named me "Boka" – fool or 'mastana' 'maverick', he replies: "Beloved, go and sit in the School of learning."

My Guru Naluda spoke sparingly. Talking dissipates energy he said. Life cannot be built on words. The question: Who builds our life? The one who is a stream of spirituality! The one who communes with his devotees in silence! My Guru Naluda's life was an island of serenity; he lived as if in serependity. He evoked vast river of spirituality flowing from his soul in joy and tranquility...

In silence he whispered to me; **go and sit in the school of learning**.

On my return home, I deliberated on those words and wondered what did he, my Master, mean? Which school? Where should I go to learn? In those days I used to teach at the college in Calcutta. I was a Professor who was teaching 300 students. The intellectuals of Calcutta, Professors, Lawyers, Judges and the affluent gentry would sneak in the college, incognito to listen to my lectures. Needless to say, that this gave me a sense of pride. I felt elevated. So naturally, when my Guru asked me to attend the school, I was puzzled. What was his message? Which school had I to attend? And where had I to go to get that learning? Slowly and gradually wisdom dawned on me. I realised that my school of learning was Satsang. I reaffirmed to myself, that my Guru wishes that I learn the basics of Spirituality in Satsang. That I assimilate the mystic experiences gained there in and then contemplate on them, meditate on them, until my entire existence was filled with the ecstasy of that experience.

With this realisation I began to attend the Satsang with a single-minded devotion. But being immature, I did not grasp the meaning of the proverb:

> Those who melt, are moulded easily.
> Like Gold, which gives more shine with burnishing?

Those who are in true fellowship with Satsang ascend the Spiritual altitude. My Guru's Satsang was unique. It had among its devotees, Scholars, College students, men of wealth and social standing. Yet there was no distinction of any kind. There was no caste, class or community. In this School of learning we were all treated as one, which was an expression of the harmony of spiritual unification.

My Guru Naluda, did not make any kind of distinction among his devotees. I had come from far off Sind. I had travelled approximately 2000 miles to be in Calcutta. I was neither rich nor well known but yet he treated me with an overwhelming love.

A few days ago, I read a few lines from Shah Abdul Latif's Risalo. It brought back the memories of the times I had spent at the lotus feet of my Master. Shah says:

> *New messages have come from the prince; he asks neither caste nor identity.*
> *Those who walk on this path shall reach the goal.*

True, late in the night, a message came from the beloved Prince. You may want to know the identity of this Prince. He is the Spirituality Supreme. He is the Messiah of Mercy. He is the storehouse of light. And what is the message? He hath no caste, no creed, and no community.

He accepts all who seek refuge in him. I said to myself, my Guru Naluda is such a Prince.

My beloved never did ask the devotees their caste. The beauty of his satsang lay in perfect spiritual harmony. One of the devotees was an affluent retired surgeon, who in those days earned the enormous amount of Rs. 25000 per month. He lived in a large rambling bungalow.

One day he invited me home for tea. He said: "you are a member of our congregation. Come and have tea with me." I accepted the invitation gracefully, I went to his house. He met me with great respect. He welcomed me with warmth and love. He himself poured out the tea for me, saying that it gave him great joy to serve the tea personally. This egalitarian attitude practised in my Guru's Satsang taught me to be humble. How I wish you too adopt this same attitude in our satsang. Please give up every kind of distinction. Do not divide yourselves. I wish that you be united. There should be no gulf between the rich and the poor, or the learned and the ignorant. When you come to the Satsang, do so with a sense of *Samadhristi*. The day I find harmonious unity among the devotees of our Satsang, I will be happy and will congratulate you all. The company of my guru made me understand his spiritual teachings. **The one important lesson he taught in his School of learning was 'Be humble and serve'. Time and again he exhorted us to be humble. My gurudev himself was a picture of humility.**

What is humility? The question arose in my mind while I sat in Satsang. I observed my fellow Satsangis. Their humility stirred my heart. In fact they were too eager to serve their Master, taking care of his physical needs: some devotees washed his clothes: some brought him a glass of water to drink. Fellow Satsangis longed to do physical chores for the Master. They were in attendance on him all the time. What is the true meaning of humility? To be a menial? To be a labourer in the vineyard of God. Labour hard; to slog enough before you can claim a reward. Do something for others. Serve the people with your own hands. This concept of serving people with one's own hands moved me deeply.

One of the teachings, I have written down as, "In the School of my Beloved Guru, I learnt the lesson of **dignity of physical labour.**"

What type of education do we impart to our students in schools and colleges? We teach them wrong values. We teach children to be smart and fashionable. But in the School of my Master, we are taught to be humble; to value the dignity of manual work. This lesson learnt at the feet of the Master is invaluable. "'O' Boka, you fool. Abandon all thoughts of worldly pleasure. Let go of ego. Be humble and serve."

The following two lines are significant for those on this path: **"Remember one thing: always be a labourer in Krishna's Garden."**

•••••

Calcutta was a city of noise. I often wondered how I had stayed there for so long

Amidst all this rattle and noise, my Gurudev looked a picture of serenity. Inspired, I resolved to create a center of silence within. I learnt to be oblivious of the rattle of that metropolitan city.

My Guru possessed personal magnetism. Most of the time he lived in seclusion. He talked less, he rarely mixed with people. Early in the morning after taking bath he offered prayers. We used to join him in this daily ritual. Sometimes he gave discourses which were very short. Yet he attracted a large audience. This is what I call true personal magnetism. My Gurudev held special meetings on Sundays.

People from far off places came to attend his discourses. My beloved master was not a great orator. Other personalities from Calcutta like Surendra Nath Banerjee were far more eloquent. My Gurudev spoke less and gently. Despite this my Gurudev attracted people from all walks of life. We yearned to hear him again and again. As said earlier my Gurudev was a man of few words, so the first thing he asked of us is: "Come, let's sit in silence." And we gathered around him and sat in silence, gazing at his luminous face. It gave us immense joy. We were never tired of gazing at him. Looking into his beautiful eyes we lost track of all time, such was his personal magnetism. His few words made silence eloquent and his presence created a radiant bliss. Being in the presence of my Gurudev gave me a sense of security. Remembering this now I recall the words of Shah Latif mentioned in one of his original lyrics.

"Balochis found their Oasis in the village of Bhambhor".

My thirst for spiritualism increased after I met my Guru. Amidst the urban ethos of Calcutta, I had found an Oasis-

"In my Guru, in my beloved;
Beholding the persona of my Beloved
My eyes wept with joy."

Being with my Gurudev, his fellow devotees and other satsang gave me happiness. I felt ecstatic in the spiritually vibrant environment and remained in supreme joy and bliss till the end. My Gurudev was a man of very few words. Yet through silence he conveyed to me many a things. From his eyes a stream of light flowed which engulfed me and I understood those precious words: Go and study in the school. It became clear that the most important centre of learning for me was the SATSANG I decided to go more often to satsang and try to learn my master's teachings at his lotus feet.

I learn: Kirtan has a great significance in the evolution of the spiritual life.

My love for *kirtan* burgeoned at that point of time. That was many years ago. Our satsang was held in the evening. It was not slotted clockwise. My Gurudev used to laugh and say, "*Kirtan* is not time bound". Normally *Kirtan* is done for one or two hours. But at my Guru's place the tempo, the rhythm and the enthusiasm increased with every hour. Since the *Kirtan* was not time bound we did not fix our gaze on the clock. We went on beyond two hours. The length of time was inconsequential. The enthusiasm, the vigor and the energy were all that mattered. All the fellow devotees who joined us had great yearning for the Lord and so the *kirtan* was full of ecstasy. When will such yearning find its expression among our *satsangis* here?

Our Calcutta Satsang was very vibrant. It commenced with the recitation of holy verses followed by spiritual songs (bhajans) and the readings from scriptures. It ended with *Kirtan*. The *kirtan* awakened the souls of many and they wept tears of yearning. Theirs was the true thirst for god. Some of them went into great ecstasy, others fell into a swoon. This happened so often that my Gurudev had to appoint some of us to pick up these people in unconscious state, and reach them home safely.

Those who are on the path, those who yearn for God, do not bind satsang to time. If you have to slate the thirst for the Lord then you should learn to lose yourself in the *masti* of *satsang*.

Our *Satsang* had many interesting aspects. One young man would wear *khol* (Dholki) around his neck and would beat the drum. Occasionally someone played sitar. How I wish that here too in our satsang a young boy or a girl would play the melodious tunes on sitar or keep the beat on drums. In our Calcutta satsang we recited the *Kirtan* mantra *Hari bol, Hari bol, Hari bol bhai* to the accompaniment of *ektara* or *sitar*. It often happened that as the crescendo of singing voices rose higher and higher, strumming the chords of our yearning souls, we lost our consciousness. According to my Guru: *Kirtan* should contain very few words: may be one two or three words should be sung but with deep emotion. As I reflect on my Guru's words now, my hands move to pen down the following lines:

Everything around is ephemeral: it is ashes.
Then why crave for it?
Remember the One who is Eternal.
When everything fades only the A of Allah remains.
Leave all the hustle and bustle
Cultivate the soul in silence.
The promise made, I must keep it:
With love, recite the O of Om /A of Allah.
Give up the worldly relations
Nuri hark the cry of your soul,
One day we all have to go,
Beyond mind, to heavenly abode,
To recite A of Alpha, O of Om.

Calcutta was famous for rituals and long religious processions. The devotees of Chaitanya Mahaprabhu took out long winding processions, where in thousands of people joined. The people sang *Hari bol, Hari bol, Hari bol Bhai.* They sang with intense devotion. I was young then. Nevertheless I joined these processions, for I had great love for this great Vishnu saint. Carrying small flags we would exult in singing *Hari bol, Hari bol,* and *Hari bol bhai.* On more than one occasion, I was so intoxicated with the mantra that I fell in to the state of unconsciousness. Even in that delirious state I would continue to recite the mantra *Hari bol, Hari bol,* and *Hari bol bhai.* The flag would fall off my hand and I would collapse on the ground. Then the devotees would pick me in that delirious state and reach me home. They would fan me to give me air. I would be in the unconscious state of mind for an hour, two or three. On gaining consciousness, I would ask in wonder: where am I? The whole experience was mystical. I would be moved to the point of tears, I would weep again and again. Those devotees would ask me, why do you cry? How could I tell them about the inner soulful experiences which melt body, mind and the soul? The experiences which were an answer to the cry of my soul? Some people wondered how I could be unconscious for an hour or two and wake up with fresh lease of energy and vigour. They asked me: How I fell into a deep swoon? Why I became unconscious? How could I convey to them my soulful experience of joy and bliss?

To evade their questions I would say: "Chaitanya Mahaprabhu". Most of the time I kept quiet. In silence, vivid thoughts flowed into my mind. It was beloved Chaitanya Mahaprabhu who gave to the people the beautiful mantra of Hari Bol. His message, his mantra of two words is sufficient in this Kaliyug to redeem you of your misdeeds. Recite this mantra everyday and be blessed.

These processions were taken out on Sundays. Large number of students, young men and women and children, grouped together and moved about in the streets with one voice, *Hari Bol Hari Bol Bhai*. Recounting those experiences, even now I am moved to tears. I shed tears of nostalgia. I look within at the beautiful picture of Chaitanya Mahaprabhu indelibly imprinted on my heart and I rejoice as I bow down, seeking his blessings.

To the school of murshid the Master, I go and learn the A of Spiritual Alphabet. My dear, learn this lesson of Spirituality; recite the A of Alpha, again and again. I still ask myself: What does A of Alpha mean? It means the highest, it means Iswar, OM, Allah.

One day, I ask my Gurudev, "How do I learn A of Alpha?"

His answer is, " go and sit in silence".

In silence I ask myself who am I?

The question that keeps me bothering in the hour of silence again and again is: who am I?

Very often I used to be confused and perplexed, shedding tears in silence, I kept asking myself: who am I? What is my goal?

One day, I receive the answer: I am a wanderer.

Subsequently, the three stages of AWARENESS become clear to me.

1. In the first stage of awareness, I learn- I am a wanderer.

I have wandered from one birth to another in the cycle of birth and death. If this is my fate then the same must be yours. The very thought brings tears to my eyes. I have roamed aimlessly. This is the first stage of awareness. Its makes me weep. You too should shed tears, lest they form an ocean within.

2. In the second stage of awareness I discover, "I am a yatri, a pilgrim; I must not roam and go astray".

This awareness came to me at the feet of my beloved Master. It was then that I realised that: **(i)** My place is at the feet of my Guru. He, who is in the company of the Guru, need not wander or roam anywhere. **(ii)** In the second stage I reaffirm to myself: Life is a pilgrimage and I am a pilgrim.

3. In the third stage of awareness, I realize that- I am but a disciple.

True enough I am only a disciple. May I learn at the feet of my master his spiritual teachings!

May I implement them in my life! May my disposition reflect it?

What is the quest of a disciple? His quest is for knowledge. During this phase of my life, my only cry was, "O Lord of knowledge! Teach me wisdom!"

4. What is my experience in the fourth stage of spiritual awareness? One day I hear a voice: You are a bird!

Ah! You have come from an alien land. Ah! I have to return to my native land. One cannot build a home on this planet earth. Everyone who visits this planet has to fly back to his native shore. Inspired by this awareness I remind myself: O! Bird! You have flown in here. You have to fly back.

Let me remind everyone of you, my dear satsangis, that we are birds who have flown in here for our earthly sojourn.

The Sindhi Sufi Saint Bedil has lyrically expressed this beautiful idea as:

O Bird! From where have you flown?
O Bird! Which is your native shore?
Fly back and return to where you belong.

Says Bedil: O' bird of another land. How have you flown to this earth? From wherever have you come, O' bird of the native land; remember you will have to fly back there. You do not belong to this world. Nor is this your country. Your home, your country is elsewhere.

Sant Kabir calls this other world, Ram Nagari. O' bird you are the bird from Ram Nagari who has strayed and flown here.

I am a bird; yet I cannot fly. I am imprisoned by desires and *'Vikar'* evil thoughts, what should I do to free myself? The answer I get is: Open your wings to fly into the sky.

One day, I go to my Gurudev. I openly ask him to guide me and help me to open the wings so that I can be a bird flying high up in the sky. What did my Guru say? "You will not be able to open your wings so easily," he said. "You need the help of knowledge and wisdom. Knowledge may show you the path. But far greater than the knowledge and wisdom is some thing else".

Hearing this I felt encouraged. I looked into the radiant eyes of my Gurudev and asked, with a thumping heart, "What is that which is greater than knowledge, wisdom and learning?"

My Gurudev answers, "My dear, it is something that is much higher than religion."

I began to think: "How foolish are we! We keep bickering in the name of religion. Religion is also a prison, says my Gurudev. Be free of this prison. Go beyond it and you shall see the **One**. Do not bother about the religions of others. Be concerned with your own faith and spirituality. The truth is that there is only one Almighty. He has different names in different places, in different cultures. Almighty is Allah, is Ishwar. The difference is of nomenclature."

The Divine light is **One**. The same light shines in all the religions.

Once again I am restless. I go to my Gurudev and request for his guidance. "Gurudev show me the way which will take me beyond knowledge and religion." At that juncture, my Gurudev used a word that stirred my heart. The word is 'longing'. My Gurudev, my beloved exhorts me to cultivate a deep longing for the Lord.

Some of our saints, Fakirs, and Darveshes call this longing as **Flame of Love**. It is the burning desire to behold the Beloved. One Sindhi brother wrote to me, requesting me not to use such intoxicating words, such as 'flame of Love' or 'fire of passion'. These are *Sufi* words a spiritual language describing the intensity of longing. Sami's slokas also use such phrases. Sami was a vendantist. His poetry breathes out Vedanta. He too freely, uses the term 'flame of love' or 'Ishq' in a true Sufi style.

'Ishq' means many things. It means love, longing, yearning obsession, madness of love. It also is the Alpha of platonic love. I realized, that to experience this magical ecstasy, I had to open my wings. This could be done only through pure, unconditional love, the Universal love. For this the dry leaves of books are not needed. What one needs is Shakti power; the life force called 'Love'.

One of our great Sufi Saints Bedil gives the message adequately.

He says: **'Thank god for the Ishq showered on thee.'**

Thank god for being blessed with this beautiful gift of longing. It is by the grace of god that one receives such a blessing. Those who have yearning in their heart are able to open their wings and fly heavenwards. Those who nurture this longing also feel the pangs of agony, for the true lover is one who sizzles in the sorrow of separation.

Our beloved poet Shah Abdul Latif describes such 'love longing/passion as sorrowful wail of wounded Hearts'.

I recall an incident here.

Many years ago in Haridwar we spotted an extremely beautiful woman dressed in ordinary old clothes. She appeared to be a widow. Widowhood had made her desperate and in anguish she cried out for her husband. Obsessed with this longing for him, she roamed the streets aimlessly searching her beloved. At every corner, at every place she asked the same question : Beloved, where art thou? Those three words of hers were full of pathos; for they were the words of longing, anguish and yearning. This beautiful woman was oblivious of the people around her. They ridiculed her saying she was a mad woman. But her longing for her dead husband remained unshaken. Her soulful cry was full of pathos, expressing the delicate emotional condition of her heart.

Shah Abdul Latif poeticizes such a condition of the heart as:

> The cry of agony tombed in a wounded heart
> unshared with others,
> Those who are crushed by the yearning
> suffer the separation in pain.

Unable to communicate their inner most emotions of longing and yearning with others, these seekers burn in the fire of passion, silently.

The question is: How does one cultivate such a longing? How does one tend the 'fire of passion'?

The first thing I realized was that this yearning for the higher life could not be acquired by reading the scriptures.

Secondly, living in Calcutta, I realized the futility of debates, discussion and deliberations. In Calcutta people often fought in the name of religion. Every religious cult tried to hoist its own flag. Seeing these clashes I came to the conclusion that it was meaningless to squabble over religion as this was against the basic principles of spirituality. All these people were prisoners of their 'belief'. I reminded myself: only the love for the Lord can free you, from the bonds of religious rituals.

I too desired to be free of the religious bindings. For this I prayed to God to shower his grace on me.

I waited for the spring of love to flow into my heart. May I request all of you not to be ritualistic. Not to have blind faith in hoary beliefs. Religious beliefs often cause conflicts. What happened to my native Sind? We were forced to migrate because of the partition of the country, which was created on the basis of religion.

How much have we suffered? May you not be slaves of such religious bigotry. May God grant you the power to be liberated from such bonds. Do not fight over the religious differences. Every religion is good, only its expressions are varied. Ram, Shyam are only different names. What is immanent is the faith that there is one God who resides in all. **The one in all beings**.

The next question that arises is how to evoke 'that' love deep within?

To reach that goal we have to take several steps.

The first step: Awake! Awake! Arise! From your slumber. Do not fall asleep! For says Shah Latif; those who fall into slumber, miss the goal(light). So be 'alert'. Be Awake!

Reading this my soul burst into a lyric, which bears the essence of the same teaching. The Poem:

> Do not fall in slumber
> Awake! Arise! 'O' forgetful one.
> The death looms large over your head,
> Yet you are in slumber!
>
> 'O' forgetful one
> Your eyes are sleepy
> Though all night you have slept;
> Folded in 'Self' in the maze of mire,
> You still don't realise
>   this world is but a dream.
>
> Ah! Look your eyes are drooping,
> You are still in slumber.
>
> You have shunned the fair face of truth,
> Clinging to the vicious desires,
> You have made friends with death,
> Ah! Your eyes are still droopy/ you are still asleep.
> Wake up.

Stuck in the mire of mundane affairs,
You will not heed the call,
You lost the golden chance, for a useless penny
Your eyes are closed, you are still asleep.
Wake up.
Immersed in the ebony darkness of world,
You missed the Divine light
Even now it is not too late: Heed the call,
Ah! Your eyes are still misty, you are still asleep.
Wake up.

O' man, if this be your condition then be sure: your boat has tilted with the tide. How will you proceed ahead 'O' fool? You have wasted your precious human birth. O' dear; now heed this cry and open your eyes. How long will you be immersed in dark ignorance. Awake! Awake! My voice is feeble but the cry of my anguished heart is: Awake! Awake! Awake! Heed it my dear ones.

From time to time I visited my Gurudev requesting him for spiritual guidance. The one lesson he taught me was: *open the window of your heart*. Sitting at his lotus feet amidst all the tumult, shouts and cries of vendors, and groups gathered in the street. I try to imbibe the lesson: Open the window of your heart. When the wings are open and you learn to fly, when you fly high above and look down and around you; You wonder, how could these trinkets of life, those small things give pleasure? How could I be so earth bound? I ask myself.

Shah Abdul Latif has said: "Seek the corners of your heart. Do not stray afar; for the friend you are seeking is within. There is no need to wander because, within us lies the Reality: Soul!"

Be not a vagabond. Your true friend, your beloved resides within you. Your search should be within. There the Lord, your beloved awaits you. I try to practise this lesson.

Nevertheless, one day I go to meet my Gurudev. I put the question to him, "Sir, kindly enlighten me on how to open the window of the heart?"

He replied: "The search within does not need teachings. Abandon all desires. Awaken the *Bhakti* within."

In the city of Calcutta, I gradually learn the lesson of *Bhakti*. I urge those of you on the spiritual path, to awaken the *Bhakti* within.

Again one day I ask my beloved Gurudev, what is **Bhakti?** What are its attributes?

Bhakti my Gurudev said, has the following attributes:

1. The first thing is to sing the name of the Lord with deep devotion.

    Those desiring to follow the path of *Bhakti*, should first learn to sing His holy name, and rejoice in it.

2. The second thing is to praise the Lord; sing His glories.

Like, 'O' Lord! You are merciful; 'O' Lord you are compassionate!

You have lifted the sinner from the sin; the criminal from the evil. 'O' Lord! With your mercy, you have relieved the broken men of sorrow; the unhappy of their miseries. You are the great Benefactor and the Protector of all the living creatures.

You must applause the never-ending glories of the Lord.

As Sri Krishna says to Arjuna in Gita: " O' Arjuna! Infinite is my glory!" Count a few of his blessings and acknowledge them with gratitude.

Gopis were obsessed with such longing. Who were Gopis? As the story goes, Gopis were the sixty thousand Rishis of ancient India. It is also said that when Sri Rama was banished to the forest, thousands of Rishis living there, yearned to have a glimpse of Him. These very Rishis took birth as Gopis, the milkmaids who were crazy with yearning for Shyama. How I wish I could get a grain of that crazy Love-Longing!

What is *Bhakti*?

To understand it, I went to my Gurudev again. His only answer was: open the window of your heart. **Cultivate the soul.**

There are people who develop their minds through education. They acquire academic degrees but their spiritual awareness is narrow and limited. Therefore my Gurudev reaffirmed: *Bhakti* is emotional. It comes straight from the heart.

What if you worshiped at a thousand temples? That worship is external. Go within and nurture the heart, my Gurudev would cajole me.

The question arises: How to cultivate the soul? How to awaken it?

The answer is the same: have yearning for the Lord.

Bhakti should be like an oyster. An oyster longs for fresh rainwater, and feels restless until it gets it. True *Bhakti* is a longing of that kind. A true Bhakta perpetually longs for the glimpse of the Lord.

The Sindhi famous Sufi Saint Sami in one of his *slokas* has said: "The fish is breathless, cannot live without water, water is a sustainer for the fish. Just as the fish cannot live without water, similarly a true *Bhakta* longs for the Grace of God."

What is the secret of a true devotee? It is longing. Each one of us should ask the other, do I really long for the Lord? Do I weep in my yearning for Him?

Shri Ramakrishna Paramahansa was of the belief that our yearning should be touched with tears. If you yearn for the Lord and weep with devotion, I assure you, you will be closer to God, and you will be showered by His blessings.

"O' Boka ! You 'fool' " I reprimand myself, "If you want to open the window of your heart then, learn to long for God with devotion; with *'Bhakti'*."

Because I am an ignorant fool, I keep admonishing myself. What have you learnt? You have yet to learn the prime lesson of silence. Restless, I put the second question to my Guru: "After opening the window of my heart, how should I awaken the longing?"

My Gurudev with love and patience explains it to me:
(1) The first important thing is to go into silence. Find a quiet place or a corner in a room, which has soothing vibrations, so that you can sit there as long as you like. Complete all your essential jobs, then whenever you feel like going into silence, go to that corner and rejoice.

(2) My second question to my Guru is: What is silence?

My beloved Guru smiles sweetly and replies: "Boka, silence is of three kinds,

(a) The first is the silence of 'Activity'. Stop all activity and remain in silence for as long as you can. Let not mundane thoughts disturb the tranquility of your mind.

(b) The second is silence of memory. Past has a habit of crawling into the present. When we sit in silence, unhappy events, adverse remarks, and unkind behaviour swim into the present memory. Learn to stop the flow of thoughts arising from the past. Be in the 'Now'.

(c) The third is the silence of desires. Every one of us is a prisoner of desires. This silence is very difficult to obtain. Rishis moved deep into the forest and practised *tapasya* but alas, they too could not silence the vast sea of desires. One must quell the desires, be firm with one self and avoid being a prey to the passions.

To practise these three types of silences, we need the Grace of a Guru. Without his grace it is difficult to take even a step forward on the path of spirituality. I pray for that grace.

I learnt my spiritual lessons at the feet of my master. I tried to practise his teachings.

Nevertheless, anxiety or worry often troubled me. I would feel remorse and fall into a pensive mood. To all this my Guru said, you are an alien bird here. Hence you are restless.

Later I found the same message in a Sindhi Sufi's verse:

'You are a bird of another land.
You have to return from where you have come'.

Fly far away from the maddening crowds, from the fights, clashes, battles and wars – to the ethereal land of bliss and peace – To thy Native land. Where is our Native land? Day after day, night after night, have I pondered over it. Our Sufi Saints call Him the Infinite – beyond time and space. They also refer to His abode as 'boundless'.

"My beloved is my Universe.
How can I hold the Universe in a limited space?"

Naturally, then the question arises: how do I find this Beloved, who is beyond Time and space? Who is Infinite! He is not to be found in limited space of the world. If that were so, all the rich and wealthy people would have Him. Believe me kings and nawabs are unhappy.

"The Beloved has no length, no breadth, his dazzle is infinite.
My Beloved cares not, though my longing is deep."

O' God, you are a riddle beyond my comprehension. I yearned to solve the riddle. I checked with my Guru for a secret formula. My Guru spoke few words for he was a man of silence.

He said: "Remove the veil of ego." There was magic in those words. How does one remove the veil of ego? Have you ever pondered over your speech? How many times in a day do you use 'I'? All our talk bubbles with the one word 'I' the 'ego'. Count the 'I' and you will have measured your 'ego'. There is another word for ego. It is self, the outer self, and the 'little' self. The Higher self, the Inner self, runs miles away from the little 'self'. Give up this self-centeredness. Enter the larger portals of Higher self. Lift the veil of mist, and behold the dazzle of the Great Giver. I recall the words of a Sindhi Fakir:

The Little self will never touch the native shore.

The one who has a large size ego will not reach the Golden shore. How fortunate was I to have such a Guru! He, the spiritual stalwart taught me in silence the 'deep' lessons of self–realisation. He was Great! May I practise his spiritual lessons on this sojourn on planet earth, and be worthy of him. His kindness was so great, that I kept asking him questions, clearing my doubts and learning each day something new at his lotus feet.

In Calcutta

One day a few of my college students came to meet me. Some of them were in high positions. One of them later became the Chief Minister of Bengal. These students were very keen that I join them for a day's picnic to a garden. After much persuasion, I agreed. One fine morning, around 7'oclock we started for the garden. It was a large sprawling place. It reminded me of Shahibaug of Lahore. We strolled in this garden leisurely. When the students felt tired and hungry, we chose a corner to sit down. The students asked me, "how is that

I don't feel hungry." My students had the freedom to speak to me as a friend. After taking meals we rested for a while. All of a sudden like a bolt from the blue, dark nimbus clouds mounted the sky. They threatened to rip it open. I warned the students of the impeding cloud burst, and worse still of the on coming deluge which would devastate us. "If it rains," I warned them, " It will be difficult for us to cross the swollen waters of Ganga. So let us move out of here." The students agreed, but still lingered on for a while. I asked them to scan the sky and to read the language of the clouds. They did not heed my warning. Few drops of rain started falling, and I persuaded my students to move out. We climbed into two boats. The rain started pouring. The students, their faces crest fallen, became nervous. They hesitantly asked, "Sir, what should we do in this stormy weather?"

I told them that they did not heed my warning. They promised to abide by my advice. "Pray, tell us what should we do?" they implored. The heavy rain water filled the boat. I was disturbed. I talked to the boatman. He was a Muslim. "Tell me what does the weather say?" He was surprised. "Allah Ka Asra, Allah Ka Asra", he replied. "Man is helpless in a situation like this. It is God who is our ultimate support. He alone can save us."

I looked at the Ganges – at its swelling waters! If God willed, I shall go. All kinds of turbulent thoughts troubled my mind. May be I would be washed away by the river. It did not matter to me. I was concerned about the young students, innocent lives who had yet to step into the portals of life. What if something went wrong? Their lives were precious.

These students asked me again, "Tell us Sir, what should we do? Sir, you can save us from the watery grave."

"Not me. Prayer alone can save us."

"God will save us for your sake!" They cried.

"My dear children you are young. You are closer to God than I am." Our boats rocked on the swelling, swirling waters of the Ganges. One student, doing his post graduation, was an agnostic though he was a Brahmin by birth.

"I know philosophy. I know logic. I do not know to pray," he wailed.

"My dear children. Remain calm. Be quiet. Relax your minds. In that state of calmness close your eyes and pray with all your heart. Hare Ram, Hare Ram, Ram Ram Hare Hare. The more placid your mind, the greater the effect of the prayer." Everyone closed their eyes, including the agnostic student. We sang Hare Ram Hare Ram, Ram, and Ram Hare Hare with deep devotion.

What enthusiasm, what depth of emotion filled that prayer! The clouds began to disperse; the sky became clearer, and beautiful again. The students continued their refrain of Hare Ram till both the boats reached banks of the river safely.

Calcutta is a volatile city agog with the social and political activities. At one time Calcutta was the capital of India. It was the centre of commercial activity. Calcutta was politically alive, as is Delhi now. Calcutta was the meeting ground for politicians and social reformers. It was the venue for upcoming revolutionaries. Surendranath Banerjee, a great leader of Calcutta had a gift of the 'gab'. His oratory shook the very ground he stood on. On the other hand, there was another politician by the name of Bipin Chandra Pal, who had made in Calcutta his battleground.

Bipin Chandra Pal was a great man. I called him B.C.P the thunder. His speeches were fiery. When he spoke, it was as if the lightning had struck the sky.

While in Calcutta, I witnessed a great jubilation. One day, the whole city was agog with one cry: Lokmanya Tilak is coming tomorrow! The people, both young and old, were enthusiastic about his visit. They gathered together, to organise and celebrate the event in a big way. The city bubbled with joy. Every one was eager to have his *'darshan'*. Calcutta city did not have a hall big enough to accommodate so many people. So they gathered on the terrace of a house. I too went there, and joined the jubilation. The function was called *"Swadeshi Mela"*. Lokmanya Tilak presided over that function. The organisers had written to him at Pune, to grace the occasion, which he readily agreed. Lokmanya Tilak looked old. He had suffered ill health while in the jail. It is said those who suffer shall survive! This great patriot of India had suffered bravely and survived.

Nevertheless, he presented a picture of calmness, sitting in a beautifully decorated chair; he looked at us and bowed humbly to one and all. Another brilliant orator Surendra Nath Banerjee – the man with the Golden voice, a true patriot, who had relinquished his I.C.S post to serve the country, welcomed Lokmanya Tilak with open arms. He spoke of Tilak: "Lokmanya Tilak has come all the way from Maharashtra to bless this function."

Lokmanya Tilak delivered a thought provoking speech: "My dear brothers and sisters! Today I place before you, my belief that you are not beggars at the door of God, you are not to beg for favours. Swaraj is your birthright. Be bold. Have courage. Demand what is yours. Demand Freedom. It is our birthright, and we shall not rest till we get it. In principle I do not want to fight. But I believe in getting that which is our birth right!"

Calcutta had great attraction for me. Perhaps my real home was Calcutta. There I built beautiful relationships. I forged friendships. I learnt at the feet of my Master. I met many great men! One of them was that stalwart, Prof. Stephen. A foreigner, his love for India had brought him to Calcutta. A great philosopher and a scholar, he was highly educated – that too in England; but he was very humble; and down to the earth. The students loved him. He was reticent and spoke sparingly. His calm and concern for others made him extremely popular. Whenever we met him, he would smile. It is said those who are highly educated have less faith in God. But that is a myth. Prof. Stephen was a man of faith! Often he said: Too much learning distracts one from God!

What a great thought!!

The European Tour

It was long ago. In the year 1910, I was invited to a religious conference under the banner of WELT Congress: The congress of the world faiths.

This conference was held at Berlin in Germany. Representatives from all over the world belonging to different faiths: Christianity, Islam, Buddhism, Hinduism, Jainism and Zorastrian converged at this conference. Several years before this a similar conference of religions was held at Chicago. It was called Parliament of Religions. The Chicago Conference threw a fresh light on religion and spiritualism. It advocated peace and harmony of all faiths.

'The Chicago Parliament of Religions' is dear to all Indians, because our very own Swami Vivekananda had delivered a path breaking speech, which moved the hearts of millions. His powerful oratory and wisdom stunned the world. The Americans realised that it was foolish on their part to send their missionaries to a land, which had spiritual men like Vivekananda. They realised the futility of spending millions of rupees on missionaries, trying to convert Hindus to Christianity. It was after the success of The Chicago Conference, that it was decided to hold

a similar Conference at Berlin. Four persons from India were invited to this conference. They were:
1) Prof. Teja Singh – A world renowned scholar.
2) Principal Harmich Chandra Mitra, who headed the City College of Bengal.
3) Sri Promotholal Sen, my Gurudev: a man of simplicity, devotion and Spirituality.
4) This humble self.

I was surprised to receive this invitation. On one hand I felt I should go abroad and keep abreast of happenings overseas. On the other hand, as I sat in silence, I received the vibrations to stay back. I was still a novice and had a long way to go on the path of spirituality. I was barely 30 years old. I politely declined the invitation and decided to stay back.

My beloved Gurudev came to know of this. At that time I was in Karachi. He wrote to me. He urged me to write another letter immediately accepting the invitation. He further encouraged me with the words, 'Perhaps you feel, that you are alone; but you are not alone. I will be accompanying you to this conference. You will have no difficulty whatsoever because I shall take care of you.'

I was thrilled to bits. My Gurudev was to be with me! I wasn't worth the dust of his feet, yet he had showered his grace on me. In that moment of joy, I read a verse from Shah Abdul Latif, which was a reflection of my own happiness:

> *In spite of all my faults, he showers his Grace,*
> *Such a one is my Guru, my Guide! Says Latif.*

My beloved Guru was such a spark. He lit the path for me and took me to greater heights.

While I was preparing to travel abroad, doubts crossed my mind: who would listen to an unknown person like me? In those days, only a handful of Indians went to Europe for higher studies. The students in England and Europe were either agnostic or atheist. They questioned religion and the existence of God. They were enamoured by the glamour of Science and technology. The students were more concerned with freedom and democracy than the matters of religion and spirituality. India too was in the grip of National movement. Lokmanya Tilak gave to the nation two brilliant words Swaraj – Self-rule. The nations of the world echoed with sounds of democracy. The rationalism of the times made people believe, that Sri Ram and Sri Krishna were myths. Under those conditions who would give me an ear to hear my idea of Faith.

When in England, I continued to wear my ethnic clothes. My normal attire was Parsi trousers, coat and Zoroastrian cap. Being a proud Indian, I substituted the cap with a turban. With some difficulty, I was able to get a ready to wear turban. As I walked through the streets of London dressed in this attire, children mocked and sniggered at me. To them I looked an alien creature from an alien land. One day as I strolled in a lane, a group of children thronged me. One of them asked, what is the time please? Looking at my watch, I told them the time. The children were aghast. They had mistaken me to be an uneducated jungle man. One of them said, 'It speaks,' as if I was a strange animal. Mahatma Gandhi too when he went to England, did not change his dress. He had set an example of being a proud Indian. Before that, any one who went abroad wore Western clothes. Even our great national leaders like Surendranath Chatterjee, and Shere Punjab Lala Lajpat Rai wore Khaki hat (topi) while in England.

Within me, I nursed a secret desire: to offer a special gift to the people of the West. For me, the most precious 'gift' was the Gita and the teachings of our Rishis. Strangely enough, when I returned to India, my love for Gita and its teachings intensified. My love for Upanishads increased. I began to value our scriptures even more, as a great treasure.

Before my voyage to the west, I carried two very strong beliefs:

- Reverence for our Rishis and Spiritual Gurus.
- Immense love for the poor and humble village folks. May I ever serve the Great Masters; may I ever serve the downtrodden poor village folks, has been my prayer always.

In what capacity did I go to England? Some go there as tourists. Some go as teachers and some go as preachers. But I went there as a humble 'pilgrim'. I was barely thirty years of age, inexperienced and still a student learning the lessons at his Master's feet. Who was I to preach to the west? In Europe, I am asked: In what capacity have you come? I reply, 'I am a pilgrim here!'

My dear readers, who is a true pilgrim?

    I. He who is pure. My soulful cry to Lord was to keep me pure and unsullied.

II. He who is a spring of love. My prayer was, that I should bind everyone in love.

I recall the words of a Sufi who finds unity through love. Love is the source of the universe. This is the truth I have discovered- Love is unification. Love is immanent. I was called to the west to give them a message. What message did I give? The message of Love:

> Give love, live love.
> Lo and behold, the wonder of love
> It shines in every face: It is God!

I made certain resolutions before I left for the foreign tour.

1. I will remain simple: simple in dress; simple in speech; simple in thought.

While abroad, I met a friend Shri Bhoj Singh. He was a well-known political leader from Sukkar. A great lawyer, and a lover of *'Gurbani'*. He met me with love and affection, and cajoled me into going with him to the theatre to watch a play.

"I have bought two tickets, one for you and one for me," he said. I declined the offer with the words: 'My dear friend, please excuse me.' He was surprised; surprised that being in England, I refused to go to an English play, for which he had paid five shillings per ticket. Surrounded by such temptations, my heart still recited the beautiful mantra of *Haribol. Haribol. Haribol bhai!* Whenever left alone, I kept repeating this mantra. It kept loneliness at bay!

2. My second resolution: Not to eat flesh diet.

Reading the life story of a saint, my eyes were wet with tears. Intensely moved by the compassion of Shanti Deva I prayed to the Lord to shower his grace on me, as he had done on that saint. It was the virtue of compassion, which I learnt from the teachings of Gautama the Buddha, and Sri Shanti Deva. I therefore resolved to seek the blessings of birds and animals; to love them as my younger brothers in this one family of creation.

While in England I kept away from nonvegetarian diet, often I had to go in search of a vegetarian restaurant. In England and in Europe people were steeped in luxurious living, relishing meat and having no qualms about it. I said to myself, "I am in the wrong place. These countries are soaked in blood. People have no compassion in heart."

By the grace of God I overcame several temptations. The more exhibitionist the culture of a country, the more had I to exercise control over my senses. In this effort God did help me.

I began my foreign trip on a ship. On 24th July 1910 we reach the city of Eden. (Fourteenth July is very dear to me as it is Sadhu Hiranand's anniversary). Eden of those days was a small 'coaling' station where the ships picked up their fuel.

I went sightseeing in Eden. It is the city of Arabs. One Arab boy and a few youngsters beg for *'baksheesh'*. I gave them whatever I could. At that time too my heart was filled with compassion not only for birds and beasts but also for the poor and the lowly.

As I go around the town I notice a sign above a shop: 'Topandas'. I am sure, it belonged to a Sindhi brother. But I had little time. In Eden I saw a church with the inscription: St. Francis.

Beyond it was a cemetery. There was a huddle of houses, all painted white. I went a little further, few chaps were shouting, 'Eat Potato'. I could make out from their dress, that they were Somalis. Incidentally, Somali dress is very similar to that of Bengalis.

I did visit one more place in Eden. It was a Gurudwara where a few devotees were offering worship. Guru Nanak is ever in my memory and therefore I was delighted to be in the Gurudwara. Oh God! How kind you are to bless me in this foreign land, with your grace!

On my return to the ship, I met a white man. He blatantly asks: Do you know English? I smiled at him and nodded. He told me, "I have stayed in India for sixteen years. I find that Indians do not trust each other."

I told him he was much mistaken. He then said, "What do you know? You are a young teenager. Aren't you studying in school? The women in India are low, - unchaste!"

I felt sorry for this white English man. Even after staying in India for 16 years, he did not know the true *Bharat*. Indian women are the most chaste in the world. Their purity is legendry.

I recollect in England I was asked to deliver two lectures on 'India and Christianity'. Those lectures were held in the city of York. After the lecture, an English man in the audience stood up and said :I wish I were an

Indian! What a privilege to be born in India! At that time I thought of the English man on board the ship, who had scorned at India and her women.

The streamer moved out of Eden. I read the Holy Scriptures. Gita, Upanishads and Sukhmani Sahib. I recited with joy:

I see you everywhere
I hear your clarion call from all,
All the places belong to you! O Lord!

It was night. Moon bright and shining in the sky gave me a mystical feeling. I was overwhelmed. I yearned for my motherland. The same feeling, the same pull I experience now for my beloved Sind. Even now, when I lie down in the night I see wonderful images of my motherland. That night on the steamer too, I had the same feeling, the same yearning for my dear country India. With tears in my eyes, I recall the scene, time and again as I read Shah's verse:

My eyes are parched with pain, searching for the Lord.
Tears fall on cheeks, like rain drops,
My yearning for the One rises, even as crowds mill around.

The yearning for my motherland increased with the distance. Distance lends enchantment to the view. How true! Absence creates a void, it creates a longing difficult to describe.

I wrote a few letters home. In those letters, I have described my longing for the motherland. At that time, I was much younger and highly emotional. My longing was deep; my feelings intense. I had not been affected by the worldliness of those times. My prayer on that journey was:

> O' lord! I am a vagabond
> Do not abandon me
> O' Lord! I am lonely and forlorn,
> Do not leave me alone.
> (Lest at your door I moan)!

The British had conquered Eden in 1837. Sind was seized a few years after that, in the year 1843. Eden was a small port, with a population of a thousand people. It did not have any modern amenities. It lacked water; was very hot; yet I liked its climate. Eden has a tower with a clock. It reminded me of Hyderabad Sind. To be honest, I did not have much love for Hyderabad. I wasn't aware that we would have to leave it one day and I would pine for it with nostalgia.

Hyderabad had narrow lanes. Among them was a particularly small lane: Dalwani lane. It was so narrow that two persons could not pass through it. Our small mud house was situated there. Whenever I went out, I looked down, for I am a shy person. Some loving sisters would open the window to see this shy young man with down cast eyes! Eden reminded me of those days in Hyderabad Sind.

As soon as we sailed out of Eden, the sea became rough. The ship bobbed up and down. For a moment we were scared. I summoned up my faith in God and faith in Benevolent Higher power. The momentary storm passed away. We heaved a sigh of relief. I was overcome by a powerful emotion. Seeking a quiet corner, I sat down to be with myself and prayed to the Almighty, thanking him for manoeuvring the ship to safe waters. In those days my faith was staunch. As I scanned through the various scriptures, my mind dwells on a particular line:

'Oh creature of the earth, do not be away from the Atman!' Those who are away from the source, fall into sin, says Rishi.

How does one fall in sin? When away from God we lose control over our senses. Temptations abound. We fall prey to dishonesty, corruption and other evils. Even the educated people yield to evil desires such as greed.

I meditate on those words, I realise that the feet which God has given us, are to walk and not to crunch people, we are given feet so that we may go out and serve the poor. So take care of your feet as they have a higher purpose in life.

Similarly, I thought of eyes. Eyes see a lot of evil. Eyes drag us to temptation. When we see a beautiful form or are exposed to an obscene picture, we feel titillated. Whenever, we see a beautiful attractive form think it to be the image of God. Even my eyes can be demonic and deceptive. Hence keep your eyes focused on the *Atman*. Human mind is very restless. It gallops. It schemes. So control the mind.

What is the Ideal life? There are two words taught to us by the Rishis. *Brahma Lok* and *Kavyalam*.

What do those two words mean? They mean unification – one source – One Brahman. Those on the spiritual path should fix their mind on spiritual unity.

How to achieve oneness (Spiritual Unity)? In the Upanishads there is a word, *'Neti'*. The Rishi says: "Oh Dear, Whatever you see 'is not': neither the house nor the pride nor the ego nor the pain nor the glamour exists. It is all *'Neti'*- non existent."

Wherever you look, affirm to your self that it is only He who exists. In the rich and the poor, in the good and the bad, in the ugly and the beautiful. It is only Him.

All around is Him ! Leave your laziness and be alert!
Give up your self-centeredness,
O man, and have the vision of the great One!

Run away from limited self; from your selfish self-centeredness! Rejoice not in the transitory material things. But find the true bliss in His vision.

One night, in my sleep I dreamt of a noble soul : Mr. Pratap Chandra Mazumdar- a *Brahma Gyani*. He wrote spiritual literature. When I secured the first rank in matriculation examination, I was awarded books as prize. I was given the choice to select my books. I chose the following books:

1. The spirit of God.
2. Oriental Christ.
3. Aids to Moral character.

This noble soul lived a life of *'tyaga'* and renunciation. Although he was married, his life was as pure as that of a *Brahmachari*. This dear one travelled all over Europe and America. Wherever he went, he spoke about India's greatness. People all over the world were impressed by the beautiful expression of his thought and philosophy.

At that time there was a poet in America by the name of Whittier. I had been reading his poetry. In one of his lyrics he pays tribute to Mr. Pratap Singh: The image of Pratap Chandra floats before my eyes. I met this dear one in Calcutta during his illness. He was all praise for Sind and Sindhis. He had visited Sind and enjoyed his ride in a launch on the river Indus. I asked him: "Sir, why do you think Sindhis are wonderful people?"

He replied, "I have seen two virtues among Sindhis.
1. Sindhis are a very hospitable people. Their hospitality is exceptional.
2. Sindhis are people of great devotion. They are basically emotional. They are large-hearted people immersed in *Bhakti*.

One Punjabi brother also had the same opinion about Sindhis. He said, "You Sindhis celebrate Guru Nanak's birthday with great devotion. In fact your enthusiasm is far greater than ours."

Hence I urge you, 'O' Sindhis, do not forget *Bhakti*. It is true that we lost all our wealth during the partition. But we still carry our intrisic culture within.

It was the month of July. This month is very sacred because it is the month of Sadhu Hiranand's death anniversary. I'll place before you my schedule of 25th July. I woke up at 4.30 in the morning. At 5.30, I offered my prayers; at 6.15. I had morning tea. A young girl used to get us our morning tea but I had instructed her not to disturb me and leave the tea tray outside my door. From 7 to 8, I sat in my prayer. From 8-9 I did my mundane chores.

10 o'clock was the time for breakfast after which I used to sit in meditation. On that day I was running fever. I needed rest. It was the chilly sea breeze which had affected my body. After resting, I had my tea at 4 o'clock. From 5 o'clock to 6 o'clock I wrote letters. At 6.30 we had our dinner. (I think this tradition of early dinner is a good one.) At 7.30 in the evening I stood at the deck of the steamer. I reflected:

Oh! Ocean where are we travelling. Wherever we go. Oh! Ocean, bless me so that I bear witness to India's greatness.

The sea breeze was lovely. I retired to my room. I read for a while before going to bed. I generally slept from 11 pm to 5 am. Six hours of sleep is enough. May be for some it is less, for some it is more. But for me six hours of sleep is enough.

On Monday the 26th of July the ship arrives at Suez Canal. The Suez Canal is as narrow as Phuleli in Hyderabad Sind. Two ships cannot cross it at the same time.

We reached Port Said. Two Sindhi brothers await my arrival. They did not know me. But the list of passengers had my name. They checked it and came to receive me. Apparently they were traders and their office was near the harbour.

They checked my credentials. They told me, "We have come to receive you, and there is a shop nearby where other Sindhi brothers have gathered to welcome you." I fear that the ship may stay put for a short while. I express my fears to them. They assured me they would reach me to the ship in time. These two Sindhi brothers took me to their shop. Their love and affection touched my heart. The few Sindhis who had gathered there extended a warm welcome. I was amazed by their hospitality. I was glad to see them knitted together.

Wherever I have travelled, I have been over whelmed by the warmth and affection of Sindhis. Today we Sindhis are scattered all over the country. I pray and ask of you: Do not forget this great quality of emotional bonding. At present I feel our bonds are weak. We must survive as a community because, we are the inheritors of a great civilisation.

Perhaps you are unaware of your heritage, your achievements and your aspirations of the past.

I have great fascination for the ocean. Time and again I have watched the sea and the moon. The blend of two on a moonlit night is both magical and mystical. Even before, we arrive at Port Said; I borrowed a pair of binoculars from a fellow traveler and had a look at the city. There were modern buildings surrounding beautiful hills, presenting splendid sights; there was a lighthouse, which throws beams of light over the city. Through the binoculars, I could sight a cluster of Arabs working, breaking stones and sweating. My heart went out to them. Though they were Arabs they too are my brothers. They were very poor; probably they earned little and sweat more. Day in and day out, they broke the stones relentlessly. A thought crossed my mind: the poor have patience, their forbearance is great. It prompted me to pen down a few lines:

The patience of the poor!
The cruelty of the power!
This sinful civilisation is built on the patience of the poor people.

I implore you, do not exploit the poor. Treat them as your own. Do whatever you can do for them. The poor need food and shelter; they need sympathy and prayer. Never forget that, the exploitation of the poor is because of their patience. May you learn to serve them. Believe me, they are the images of my God! They are the pictures of the great Almighty!

Incidentally, Guru Nanak had also travelled to Arabia and left his mark there. Even today two Gurudwaras, enshrining Guru Granth Sahib exist there, and prayers are held daily there.

I was fortunate to be travelling with my Guru on the steamer. I was young and naturally my emotions were raw. I often marvel at the intensity of emotional and spiritual yearning of my younger days or was it because my Guru was by my side, that my yearning for the lord had intensified?

On the voyage, I fell ill. My Gurudev nursed me tenderly, I felt humbled. I should serve my master and not the other way round. I was struck by sea-sickness and was confined to my cabin. Within a day or two I recovered. It was the grace of God and the benedictions of my Guru.

Sea fascinates me; I gaze at the rolling waves for hours together. The rise and fall of the tide. The changing colours of the waves under the sun. To me this mysterious music of the ocean is mystical: as if it contains the secret of life.

I would sit on deck and reflect on the sea thinking: If the ocean is so beautiful, its waves so fascinating how beauteous must be the Creator of it all.

Once in a month, the passengers would gather on the deck and dance. One night while I was watching the waves from the deck, a man comes and requests me to vacate the deck. They are going to have a dance party here.

'Everyone is invited, you too come and join us,' he says. I excused myself. The man is surprised. Instead of joining the dance party, I spent the night with my Guru in his cabin room.

On the previous night I had a dream. In the dream I learnt two phrases, which my heart kept humming. The two lines are:

I am a servant at your door.
I beg love, for I love you all the more.

The ship moved out of Suez Canal and near the shores of Egypt. Egypt at our time was seat of great civilisation. It has many interesting historical stories. One such story is of Cleopatra. It is a heart-wrenching story. The story goes as: A powerful warrior, who has come to conquer the mighty Egyptian Empire. Anthony, for that is the name of that warrior who is so enticed by the beauty of Cleopatra, that he stays put in Egypt. When his people in Rome urge him to return, saying, 'the river Tiber is calling you,

Oh warrior, return home.'

He replies: 'Let the Tiber be on fire, I shall not return home.'

Just imagine the power of a woman's charm and beauty! May you and I learn a message from this. May we learn to control our passions and be true to our native land. In Egypt, I see myself on banks of a river that flows quietly. Standing on its banks, I feel tears well up in my eyes. May be the placidity of the river is superficial. Deep within, it is shaken by turmoil. May be that is what has moved me from within. On the banks of river Nile, I remember Shyam. I repeatedly called out 'Shyam'. No one there would understand and so I had the liberty to call out my beloved's name as loudly as I could. I failed to understand this yearing for Shyam on the banks of Nile, which is thousands of miles away from my homeland.

Our steamer sails by the coast of Egypt and moves into the Mediterranean Sea. I am to disembark at a port and take a train to Germany. After attending the Congress of Religions there, I had to proceed to England by train.

The steamer halted for a while at a west side Port. A woman sang and played a strange instrument. A man held an Umbrella over her head. The musical instrument is an enigma to me. It was not Sitar, for that is the music instrument of India. Sitar is a wonderful instrument, which moves you emotionally. Often I have listened to the melodious tunes of the Sitar. In Ancient Sindh we had a unique musical instrument called 'chang'. As the story goes: Bejal sang to the tune of 'chang' so beautifully that it moved Raja Diyaj to ecstasy. The Flute is also another melodious instrument, which gives out melodious notes. But what this girl was playing was very different.

It was violin. Violin has deep heart wrenching notes. This girl sang while playing the Violin. The more we heard of her, the more we were struck by her skill. We were so moved by the music, that some of us wept. I said to myself: Oh Lord bless me with the ability to hear your divine music in the depths of my heart!

As the ship sailed in the Mediterranean Sea, I go within, I hear a voice: You are yet not prepared. Prepared for what? I failed to understand.

The congress of religions was to be held at Berlin. People from all over the world – Japan, China, European countries, England and the USA have assembled there to participate. I was to present a paper at the conference. But I had not worked on my lecture. Sitting on the deck, I gazed at the waves. I sent out a small prayer to the mystical Nature. *'Tamasoma Jyotir Gamaya'*. Many thoughts come to my mind. Many ideas are conceptualised.

O Lord, the world is passing through a dark tunnel buzzing with rumours of war. War is cruel.

People are steeped in darkness; they need light; more light. They need peace, not war. How to dispel darkness? Unfortunately, the countries do not realise the tragedy of war, the devastating consequences of war! Everyone is immersed in darkness of ignorance. Again I prayed that wisdom may dawn on people, and they may be able to see the light of truth.

O God, disperse the dark clouds of war, looming large over nations. Show them the silver line. Make Politicians see sense. Lead them out of darkness into light.

Could this be the guideline of my speech? My speech for Berlin was worked out mentally, on the ship. I reached Berlin two days ahead of the conference. This is how I wanted to begin my speech:

I have brought with me the message of India. What is that message?

1) First of all, all around us is darkness and this darkness continues to deepen.

2) Secondly, the great sages and saints of India have given the message of light: For instance Gautam the Buddha gave the message to his disciple, 'Kindle the light'. Light the lamps. (Awaken thy Self!)

3) Thirdly: what is this light? It is neither electric light, nor Sunlight of the day. It is the light of the *Atman*: The spiritual Light!

The Spiritual light is the Eternal light, which never extinguishes.

4) Fourthly: How to kindle this light? How to awaken the soul? Time and again in Holy Scriptures we are urged to ignite the eternal flame. How to do so?

I wove these four thoughts into the speech for the conference.

At this point I recollect the words in Upanishads. *Mokshadwara*. My quest in this life is to open the *Mokshadwar*. The *Mokshadwar* has four sentinels. I prefer to call them four thoughts.

The first thought:
1) Self Control: If you wish to embark on the spiritual journey, then practice self control. Money, fame, name and honour are all insignificant if you choose this path. If you wish to make progress on the spiritual path then practise 'Self Control'. To this day, I pray to the Lord: May I be able to control my senses. Even when I was abroad, I prayed to God for his mercy and his grace so that I may not go astray.

The second thought:
2) *Dhyan*: Meditate, Meditate. Meditation opens up your '*Shakti*'. Mind needs to be controlled. It runs wild. It needs to be in one place. For this sit in silence at least for half an hour. Reflect and meditate, till the troublesome thoughts leave you. With meditation you will regain equanimity.

The third thought:
3) Contentment: Time and again we are faced with situations like, a friend borrows money from you, then you find out he is a cheat, a dishonest man. What is your reaction? You are angry with the man who has cheated you. You may be meditating everyday, but this kind of behavior of another person upsets you. Equanimity, patience and contentment are very necessary in life. Face life's difficulties and challenges with patience. We all go through such testing times. Let not another's behavior upset you. In Italy I learnt a good proverb. *He who has patience is lucky.*

4) The fourth thought:

Fellowship with the holy ones. Be in the company of a sage or a saint. Go and join a Satsang.

I reflected on these four thoughts. They became the four beads of my rosary. It was this rosary of thoughts that I presented in a form of a paper at the Congress of Religions in Berlin.

A man, who builds his life on these four ideals, knows that sympathy is the key to good governance. And the Brotherhood of Nations cannot be formed without the key of sympathy.

The steamer reached Naples. I hired a Victoria and went sightseeing. I was overjoyed to read a sign above a shop: Dhammal Chellaram. This is a Sindhi name; Sindhis have ventured out far and wide. Sindhi entrepreneurs are sincere, hardworking, and very cordial. That's the secret of their success.

Atlast we reached a place which is very dear to me. It is Rome. While in Rome I learnt a few words of Latin. For example, the Latin equivalent of Potato, Milk, etc. I made a list of things I needed and found out equivalent in Latin. Butter is –Bur, Meal is Pani, Biscuit is – Biscuiti, Milk is Lati. However the word for Potato was Potato and this was enough for me because I love Potatoes and can live without other vegetables. On the ship, I requested a steward to cook potatoes for me. I gave some money to him and asked him to buy some potatoes and fry them. I like ice. The word for it was Bash-Jo.

In Rome I visited St. Mary's Church. Sitting outside this magnificent church were the poor, the sick, the under nourished people. Alms were being given to them and they were being served with love, compassion and sympathy (Comforting Words).

In modern times people have different attitude towards beggars. But I beg of you all to be kind to the beggars, the poor and the sick. Serve them with all your heart. Give them love, compassion and sympathy for they are the images of God.

Inside the Roman church, there was absolute silence I haven't witnessed such silence in any of our temples or shrines. God abides in silence. The teachings of the great ones are: seek the Lord in silence. In silence shall we be.

I find devotion and faith of the members here remarkable. Our faith is tattering; our devotion is falling. It is out of Love and devotion for the Lord, that man grows in compassion and begins to serve the poor and the needy.

New India will be built in the faith and the hero worship of the sages and saints, in the devotion and *Bhakti* for the great ones!

The Cathedral I visited had pictures of saints. People were sitting in silent corners, in meditation. Normally people are restless and talk among themselves. You may chitchat but at the same time, I request you my Satsangis, learn to be still and know the art of meditation.

Rome has great schools and Colleges. It has large gardens. Rome has large halls, where the girls come in the afternoon and paint the pictures of saints. In Rome, saints are revered, but not so in England. The English scoff at the word and make a mockery of sainthood, but in Rome it is different. In Rome a saint is a saint.

Rome has a big play ground which can seat eighty thousand people. Many types of games are played, some of them are nauseating. I wept, when I learnt of some of the cruel sports there.

At one time Rome was famous as a sports city. These sports were played by the animals. On that spacious ground animals were brought: Elephants, Cows, Buffaloes and Wolves. These animals were made to fight. During the fight, one of the animals would get injured and fall down to die.

Alas! Thousands of people watch this sport, clapping and feeling happy.

One day, on that very ground four hundred animals were mauled dead. The crowd of spectators was jubilant. The thunder of their clapping could be heard well beyond the gates of Rome, outside the city.

One day, a man is brought to this ground. He is a gifted singer. He is asked to sing a song to the tune of a musical instrument. He is a slave. He sings and sadly enough, a hungry Lion is brought to the arena. It tears the man to pieces and eats him up. The spectators, throngs of people, feel jubilant and clap merrily. Alas! The western world is obsessed with physical prowess. Muscle power is applauded. This is not to deny the existence of the compassionate and the merciful human beings in Europe. However, it is true, that in politics and in administration, western nations consider 'power' above everything else.

In day-to-day affairs, the western culture is superficial as it attaches significance to outer material things.

I hope and pray that we here in India grow in sympathy. That we live in harmony with one other. May we build a new nation on pillars of sympathy, compassion and spiritual harmony.

Another big city that I visited is Milan in Italy. Milan has many beautiful marble sculptures, many of them of Jesus Christ and other Christian saints.

In India, near Pune, we too have a city by the name of Goa. Goa has many churches, the most prominent being the church of St. Francis Xavier! St. Francis Xavier was a learned man. He was a scholar. However, an inner voice tugged at the strings of his heart. What if you have achieved name and fame? What if you are a great scholar? These questions made St. Xavier to introspect within. He decided to leave Italy. He embarked on an unknown journey to the east, to spread the message of his master-Jesus Christ. (St. Francis Xavier lands in Goa. He spreads the message of love and compassion, the two great teachings of Jesus Christ).

St. Xavier before embarking on his journey spent some time in Milan. He saw students everywhere. But he was unhappy at the type of agnostic education they received. He took up a metal gong, walked the streets, and ringing the bell he shouted: Oh dear ones, the beloved of my master Jesus, do take education, learn, but learn that which will take you nearer to thy Lord! Come Oh children and youth, come to me, I will give you true schooling. I will teach you the way to the Lord! Remember that even if you gain the whole world, you will gain nothing for you cannot get true bliss and true happiness! As I walked the streets of Milan, I remembered his call to the youth of his country.

At last I reached Berlin in Germany. Berlin is the capital city and the meeting of Congress was to be held there. It was Sunday August 7, 1910. At the station, we were received by a group of organisers. There were many such groups at work at the station. Yet, there was silence. Everyone worked quietly; peacefully. The railway stations in our country are very noisy. Berlin railway station is big, and has many workers. Yet there was silence.

I had a small suitcase and a bedroll. My Gurudev also had a small suitcase and a small bedroll. We were unaware, that in Europe, one carries one's own luggage. We were also unaware that coolies were very expensive. We handed over our luggage to two coolies, who were well dressed, wearing a complete black suit. It is ironical, that at that time I too was wearing a black suit very similar to that of the coolie!

We checked for the rates and we were to pay one shilling for each luggage. We changed our currency into 'marks' and paid the coolies their dues.

We asked these 'gentlemen' coolies to take us to a hotel. They took us to one of the most expensive hotels. In those days, only the very rich, affluent and royal Indians travelled abroad. Therefore, naturally, they took us to one of the better-known hotels. I checked into one room and my Guru checked into another room. I could not sleep during the night, because I was not used to such luxuries. The bed mattress was very soft, the quilt beautiful. I was used to sleeping on the hard floor. For years together I have slept on the floor. I was put in a room, which normally is given to Kings, Queens, ministers and rich Landlords!

I woke up early. Beams of sunlight flowed into my room. I felt happy, for even in those days, I used to worship the Sun.

I used to say the Sun is a tremendous *Shakti* of the Lord Almighty. Bowing down to the sunbeams creeping through the window, I worship the sun, and seek its blessings. Then I sit in silence and pray in my own devotional way:

Forgetting all evil,
Do your Karma,
With love in your heart, follow Dharma.

This small prayer of three lines is enough for me. Although I was very tired, I desired to go around sight-seeing in the city. After my breakfast, I sauntered around to see and feel the ethos of this city. Berlin at one time was a small village of fisher folks but had now grown into the capital city of Germany. Our dear city Karachi was also once a small fishing village, but gradually grew to a prosperous and a famous town.

The man responsible for developing Berlin into a magnificent city was the warrior King, Fredrick the Great. Germans are very proud of this King.

In Berlin City, I saw two statues. One was of Fredrick, the Great. Germans are full of praise for their King.

They say: It is true that King Fredrick the Great had many shortcomings. However, he had one great virtue. He allowed freedom of expression. His subjects enjoyed this freedom and expressed their ideas and opinions in public speeches. I wish and pray that this freedom should be given to everyone, in every country of the world. I believe in freedom of expression.

2) The other important man in Berlin, held in high esteem and whose statue is prominent is Bismark. He was an astute statesman.

After seeing these two statues, I wished to meet a person on the spiritual path; someone who had integrated body, mind and soul and lived in perfect spiritual harmony. One name that flashed through my mind was Goethe. I went out in search of him. I learnt that Goethe used to shed tears of devotion; he used to weep in the night. Berlin had many eminent personalities, experts from fields as varied as engineering and politics; experts who helped to build this powerful city into a place for commerce, trade and business. But to me Goethe alone was important.

As I go walking along the streets, I sight a signboard with the words 'Goethe'. I realize that Germans love this humble man, whose essays and poems had touched many hearts in Europe, America and Asia. Our Ancient Rishis were singers, poets and also mystics. Goethe also falls into that category. I was delighted to be in Germany. For it is the country of Goethe. I shed tears of joy as soon I stepped on the shores of Germany. And I wrote:

Ah! Today my eyes are blessed with beautiful sight!
Tears of Joy drop on the cheeks, untold!

That day, I remembered Goethe and wept in his memory.

Germans have scientific nature. It was therefore in order of things to find Academy of Sciences. Berlin has another wonderful Institute: The seminary of Oriental languages. You will be surprised to know that many Germans learn Sanskrit. Many of them are scholars of that language. I had taken Sanskrit in B.A examination. But realized my ignorance of this ancient Aryan language when I was in Germany. I had a dialogue with some of the professors of Sanskrit language. Germans have special memory for our ancient Rishi culture. Their scholarship of this ancient language is praise worthy.

I went to meet one such scholar professor. He was sitting in a small room amidst piles of books. He was wearing spectacles and was engrossed in his research work. Years later, this great scholar was invited by Rabindra Nath Tagore to Calcutta. The name of that scholar is Prof. Winternitz.

One of his books, describing Indian Culture has been translated into English. It is a great work and Rabindra Nath Tagore invited him to be in Shanti Niketan.

The Seminary of Oriental languages has scholars and Professors of Sanskrit, Persian, Arabic and a few other languages. It had students from all over the world. I was delighted to be in a country which held Indian Culture in such a high esteem.

You will be surprised to know that the conference commenced at 12 o'clock midnight. It was customary in those days to hold conferences during the night. My Gurudev and I attended this inaugural session. A chosen few delegates were invited for this session. This was a special inaugural session where the overseas delegates were being felicitated. As per the etiquette the person felicitated had to speak a few words of acknowledgement. My Gurudev was asked to say a few words. But he refused. Himself a shy person, he requested me to speak instead. In my self-opinion, I considered myself to be very shy. But perhaps that was my ego. My Gurudev was truly very shy and very reluctant to come in front of the audience. He therefore urged me to say a few words of acknowledgement. I considered it irreverent to speak in the august presence of my Gurudev. I cajoled him, coaxed him and begged of him to spare me this act. Yes, many times I would debate with my Guru. At last he agreed to say a few words. True enough his speech was very short, but it was full of wisdom. I give you the essence of his speech:

Many great scholars have gathered here to participate in the conference.

1. First of all, whenever there has been a renewal of religion, or a great regeneration, it has happened on the Asian continent.
2. Secondly, there have been many awakeners of humanity. I will mention only three.
   a) One is Buddha; I know Buddhism has found followers in Germany.

b) Two is Krishna. Unfortunately, he is unknown in this part of the world. Perhaps, it is our mistake. We have not projected him well and therefore have failed to spread his message of Gita to the world.

c) The third is Christ.

May you all follow the teachings of these three great spiritual leaders.

3. Thirdly, these three great leaders, of whom two belong to Asia, have brought the religious awakening in the world.

4. Fourthly, the Asian religions have spread into the European countries. Take a dip in these waters of the Spirit, flowing into your continent and rejuvenate yourself and make your life beautiful.

5. Fifthly, remember, by love alone shall ye attain.

Alas! We fight in the name of religion, we quarrel. We debate, and deliberate in the name of religion. Many wars have been fought in the name of religion. But remember love is larger than life. Love is God. Hate should be replaced by love.

May we all learn to live in harmony and peace. May we imbibe the message of my Gurudev and love one another.

Do not criticize any religion. Keep this one ideal before you: only through love and love alone can you reach God.

Two more people from India attended this conference. One was Principal Moitra, from a renowned College in

Calcutta. The other was Prof.Teja Singh, who represented the Sikhs of India. He was well versed with *Gurbani* and was a revered professor who later became the Principal of a College.

In those days the newspapers carried photographs of the speakers along with their speeches. Many journalists requested me for a photograph but I did not have any with me. The journalists requested me for a photo session. I excused myself. *'Photo Kum Khoto'*: Photo is a fantasy – an illusion.

An editor of a well-known newspaper of Germany requested me for a photograph. I politely declined to oblige. Next morning I found a short report and two snaps printed along with it carrying the caption in German: Prof. T. L Vaswani and his son. I was surprised and amused for I have no son. I studied the photo and found it had no resemblance to me either. Later I learnt, it was the photograph of Prof.Teja Singh and his son. This kind of irresponsible journalism disturbed me.

The speech I delivered at the conference has been now brought out in the form of a book titled 'Atam Gyan' (Atmagyan).

I will give you the gist of that speech.

The keynote of my lecture was: Reverence for self; reverence for Atman.

Time and again, I have recalled the teachings of ancient gurus and Darveshes of Sind. They all say one thing: Know thyself. What are we? Who am I? I am the shrine for the Atman. If you realize this one truth, then your life will be illumined. And all your evil thoughts will vanish. You will not wander in the maze of Maya. Nor would you compare yourself to those above you in status. Why do you run after the shadow, when you yourself carry the light within. Do not be slaves of those in authority. Do not subjugate yourself to those possessing power. Do not beg for favours. Do not grease the palms of your fellowmen for petty things like promotion in job, raise in salary or for titles and monies. You are rich in Spirit. You, who are light within yourself. Why should you flounder in darkness?

Truly a Sufi Saint has said: if you know the worth of self, you will be the victorious soldier.

My dear brothers know the soul within you; feel its greatness. See its light. Experience your infinite consciousness. Do not be enamoured by those in authority and power. Do not be swayed away by those in limelight. Do not feel inferior to those who are better off. Perceive your own individuality, you who enshrine the *Atman*.

> In six lines may I share with you my thoughts:-
> Give up your pride and ego,
> Close the chasm of hate with love,
> All that you seek is within you,
> Remember, Sikander the great,
> Conqueror of the world,
> Left behind everything.
> So dear, it is better to conquer yourself
> Be the ruler of your mind.

Be the Sikander of your Persona. Conquer yourself. Only the Almighty is the Lord. The crown prince of your quest is your eternal self, only know thyself. This message is the need of the hour even today. Because men and women are unable to meet the challenges of life, they are unable to cope up with trauma or crisis. Consequently, they feel weak and defeated. If you would know thyself, you will feel strong and healthy.

The main theme of my speech was Reverence. I placed before the Berlin Congress: Rich or poor, happy or miserable, everyone has the soul, which is Godly; hence reverence for self is essential.

Reverence is of three kinds:

1) Reverence for self, for one's soul, for one's Eternal Spirit within. Hence know your worth (You are invaluable).
2) Reverence for all that is around us, for eg. I am surrounded by you. It's my duty to respect you, to revere you.
3) Reverence for those below you. The poor, the needy, the hungry, the unhappy, the destitute, the birds, the beasts, the insects, we must have reverence for all of them. I should treat the animals and birds with compassion. I should serve the poor and the hungry. They may seem materially poor, but they are reflections of my own Self.

One day I was strolling in a suburb of Berlin. I was in search of a vegetarian restaurant. It is here that I met a student from India. I enquired with him, how he came to be there. He replied he had come there to eat food. I asked him his name. I happened to know his father, who was an engineer. I asked him, if he ate non-veg food. He replied in the affirmative saying, it is difficult to live in Europe without taking non-veg food. I further enquired of him, whether his father had taken any promise from him before sending him to Germany. He said, "Yes, my father is a religious person; he prays before taking his meals. He took a promise from me, that I would not touch food without doing pooja and I would not touch non-veg food either. Unfortunately I have not been able to fulfill these promises."

There upon I confronted him by telling him, that his father had spent so much money on his foreign education and he had not kept his word!

The student was sincere and sensitive. Moved by my words he wept. Thereafter we entered into conversation. He asked me, the purpose of my visit to that suburb of Berlin. I told him, "I come here to eat vegetarian food." This student of engineering bows down and touches my feet. He genuinely felt sorry. He promised to live by his father's word. He also realized that compassion is the root of all religion.

•••••

I was in Paris. I hired a taxi to see Paris by the night. I was surprised. Even at that late hour the city was throbbing with life. It was 12 O'clock. The restaurants, the public places, the residential quarters were pulsating with activity. There was wine and food, dance and music and joy de verve! Even though the music was pleasing, and there was vibrancy in the air, it lacked the spiritual core. The entire ethos was exciting and sensuous. I felt despondent. The common feeling of Parisians; why not enjoy the pleasures of life? The same trend of thought had travelled to India by the time I had returned.

•••••

In London I met people from all strata of society. The first lecture that I delivered there was at the sacred place of the great English man, StopFord Brooke. The topic of my lecture was 'What Europe needs'. The very topic angered some people. How could this young chap teach us what Europe needs? True, there were a few who appreciated me greatly.

There were others who thought I was too audacious to touch such a topic.

This lecture was attended by many scholars. God gave me the strength and the courage to speak. My speech:

My dear brothers and sisters, You are running after power You are running after self-pride. Pride hath a fall; and power corrupts. Europe needs simplicity and not high handedness. Any nation or an individual, any country or a community, seeking authority and power will one-day collapse.

What Europe needs is simplicity of life, of dress, of food and of simple lifestyle. I cited the example of Leo Tolstoy of Russia. How this noble feudal Lord changed. He was affluent, and a powerful, feudal Lord. But by the grace of God, he forsakes his luxuries in exchange for a simple mystical life. Leo Tolstoy comes down to the level of peasants. He wears simple clothes, forsaking all authority. He lives a humble life. Europe needs simple people like Leo Tolstoy.

"Who are you?" The question makes me think.

"I am a fool!" I reply.

"How come?"

I smile back.

"What is your goal in life and what is your ideal in life?"

"I want to be a Moth."

"How come?"

"Because a Moth desires to burn in the flame. I too desire to extinguish my ego in the quest of Eternal Flame."

Elsewhere I am asked different questions.

The question:

Which path do you advocate?

The answer:

The path of humility.

'Be like grass, which even when devastated does not complain, but merges with the earth. Be humble. Be dust." I explain.

Many years later while reading Sachal's poetry I came across the same thought. He says: "I met my Lord in leaves and grass."

I am requested to stay on in England. However I decline, saying that I can spend only sometime but to India I must return. For my spirit is linked with the spirit of India. My soul is linked with the soul of India.

I continued to stay in England for a few months. I was well looked after. My hosts took care of my every need with love and affection.

Everyday I had a session with the English scholars and laymen as well. I would discuss with them the great English poets, Shakespeare and Lord Tennyson. These sessions were very effective. At the end of every session we would hug and shed tears of joy. The whole scene was very moving.

The love and sincerity of my hosts amazed me. Often I was invited to their homes to meet their families. I was even invited by them to stay at their homes. They had enfolded me in their love. I accepted their invitation in humility, and I agreed to go to stay with a few of them. I was in the habit of waking up early in the morning. The young ones in my host families would wake up early and serve me bed tea. I had the habit of going to the prayer room and lock it from inside. I did not want to be disturbed by the young girls who served morning tea. I did not want a young sweet girl to enter my prayer room and pull me into mundane conversation. The girls were so loving and affectionate that, I became apprehensive of their intrusion. I thought it better to skip my morning tea than to have them hovering around me. This was difficult as I am a tea drinker. I requested the host girl, "My dear child do not take the trouble of getting me morning tea." She politely said, "As you wish." "What about the 'Dhobi' list?"

I told her she could bring it to me later in the day.

I stayed in England for a while. I met a scholar who had great affection for me. He praised me, saying that the girls were crazy about me. They hadn't seen a man of such pure love and radiance. He asks a vital question: What is the purpose of life?
What is the ideal of life?

Pray, tell us in simple words. The question is a direct one. The answer too had to be simple and direct.

I told him, "The purpose of life, is life itself."

This man wanted the answer in two simple words. I gave him those two simple words. Awake! Awake!

The people seated there were stunned, a young girl whose devotion for me was praise worthy, fell unconscious. The words had gone direct to her heart. After a while she regained consciousness; she tried to understand the meaning of those words. I pray, that the same words cast a spell on you. With folded hands, I pleaded, "Look within. Awaken the *Atman*, which is your true self."

For a few days, I visited the city of Bristol. Mr. Carpenter, God's good man met me. He was the principal of the famous Mansfield College, Oxford. Mr. Carpenter was an ideal teacher, very popular among students. During the course of our conversation, he asked whether I know of a famous Indian, who was in Bristol, and passed away there. I told him yes. Raja Ram Mohan Roy. He was a great social reformer. He fought the evil of Sati in Bengal. Sati is a barbarian custom, which forces a widow to burn herself on her husband's funeral pyre. Raja Ram Mohan Roy succeeded in enacting the Abolition of Sati Act.

Principal Carpenter asked me whether I wished to visit the Samadhi of this great one. The Samadhi was at some distance away from the Bristol town. He organized our visit and accompanied me to Raja Ram Mohan Roy's Samadhi.

Raja Ram Mohan Roy's Samadhi is in a quiet secluded place. It is covered by a beautiful tree, the branches of which are spread out. The care taker of the Samadhi met us with great respect and requested me to look at the visitors' book. Many well known Indians' signatures were there. Our visit to Raja Ram Mohan Roy's Samadhi was like a pilgrimage to a holy place. If at all you visit Bristol, do not forget to visit this serene place.

I sat in silence for a while and meditated before writing in the visitor's book. What thoughts did I pen? I wrote Ram Mohan Roy is lonely.

I added, His message unto you, my countrymen is: "Unite and build!"

Even today India's greatest need is for integration. May we all live in peace and harmony and rejuvenate this land with the Unity and Love.

Unite and build was the message to Indians to build India.

In Bristol I stayed with a very pious and a noble sister. This lady who had heard me was very keen to be my host. I was hesitant, but she insisted. Later I found out that she was the sister of the commissioner of Sind. On my return to Karachi, I received a note from the commissioner, inviting me to his home. I learnt that his sister had written to him about me. I did go to meet him. He asked me rather a difficult question. He said, "I have heard so much about you. I ask you what gift, what honour, what state award, what title would you like to have? If you need money and affluence, I can bestow that upon you."

I smiled and put him in a quandary. "I need nothing."

He repeated, "Do ask for something." But my reply was the same: I need nothing. He was both surprised and amazed. We maintained cordial relations so long we were in Karachi.

I was asked by many young women, "Who is your beloved? We would like to meet your beloved!"

During my England yatra, I was once staying with a family comprising of a brother and a sister. The sister would ask, "Who is your beloved? I would like to meet your beloved. To be frank with you, you are my beloved. So I am keen to know who is your beloved!" This young sister was barely twenty years. Her brother had trade links with Egypt. He was busy the whole day; inspite of which he made it a point to be at home for lunch. The first thing he would enquire of his sister was whether she had eaten her lunch. Invariably she would reply, "I am waiting for Mr.Vaswani to come." Such wonderful was her devotion for me.

Time and again she and her friends would put the same question, who was my beloved? I would reply shyly: "My beloved is Krishna. My all is Krishna."

Wherever I went in England, I carried my beloved Shyam with me in my bossom. It was in that spirit of longing that I spent my days in England. I knew those who were brought up in the tradition of English education, would mock at me. Krishna? The one who plays truant with the Gopis? But that is not the Krishna of my soul. My Krishna is the one who shook the whole Bharat; the one who gave India the beautiful scripture of Gita. My Shyam is the one who played

melodious notes on the flute and brought joy to the wilting hearts of this world.

In Bristol I was asked to visit an orphanage. That orphanage housed thousands of parentless children. George Miller, the well known writer, looked after it. George Miller was a poor man, but his life was rooted in faith. At first he opened a small orphanage in his own house. He had the conviction that God would meet his needs, whenever they arose. His prayers were answered. "Do you know why our prayers are not answered? Because we are selfish. Our disappointments are many because they arise out of our own ego. If we pray with faith and deep devotion, then God will respond and fulfill our needs."

After Bristol I returned to London. Some of the British who had heard me in Bristol and liked my lectures also came to listen to me in London. A British woman was so impressed by the talk that she invited me to stay with her, promising to serve me vegetarian food.

I went to stay in a small town in England. People here were pious and devoted. Every Sunday they get together and pray. In one such meeting, I was asked a few pertinent questions.

Q: We believe that Sri Krishna prevails upon the whole of India. Is he a major influence on the people?

Ans: I think Sri Krishna and his teachings of Gita have influenced many lives.

Q: If that is so, then what about Muslims? Are they too influenced by Sri Krishna? Does Muslim culture also exist in India?

Ans: Of course there is Muslim culture in India. There

are many Muslim writers, poets, and scholars who have enriched Indian culture.

Q: Has Sri Krishna influenced Muslim literature?

Ans: I think even Muslim writing and Muslim thought in India, reflects the humane values of Gita.

Q: Give us the proof. Can you quote any poet or any writer, who has been influenced by Sri Krishna and his teachings?

Ans: I come from Sind; the land of Sufis and Fakirs. There are many Saint Poets in Sind and Sri Krishna has intoxicated some of them.

Q: Can you name one?

Ans: Bedil.

Q: What does the name Bedil mean?

Ans: Bedil means the one who has given away his heart. There might be many such poets, but Bedil's intoxication is unusual. Sings he:

> *One experience, one mystery; enough for me to lose myself!*

On that one experience he meditated and lost all that he had. Intoxicated he loses his heart to one Beloved.

Love is such a thing. You lose yourself in the Love for another. Bedil also was lost in the love for Krishna. To illustrate the point, I quote here:

> Today is blessed! Today Shyama has come with his wonderful music,
> His beautiful face, his graceful body,
> His blue colour skin, wearing bright clothes,
> A picture of joy,

Shyam comes dancing as he moves,
Through life's sorrow filled Bazaar.

Bedil trudges through the narrow lanes of poverty and rejoices in love.

Sri Krishna had come to spread the radiance of love and dispel the darkness of sorrow from the world.

A Muslim girl by the name of Taj was also enamored by Krishna. Taj lived in Mathura, the native place of Lord Krishna.

Spreading rainbow colours
Ebullient and innocent
You rule our hearts as a King
She sings:
Darling of Nand, thrasher of Kansa.
O' of Brindavan, Beloved Krishna you are our Ruler.

Such is Sri Krishna. A rare beauty of charismatic love and stealer of our hearts. Yet his heart goes out to the poor and the lowly.

Taj was full of love. This Muslim girl was absorbed in the love of Krishna. She was attracted like a magnet by the charisma of Krishna. If we could be like Taj and rejoice in the glory of Krishna; we would consider ourselves to be fortunate.

At one such meeting, I translated a *sloka* from Gita, and explained it to the members there. They were surprised. After the sermon, many members from the congregation met me and asked me in what language did I recite. They wanted to learn that language because phonetically, it sounded very sweet. It was Sanskrit and I told them that Sanskrit was a difficult language to learn.

No doubt it was a great language. They wanted to know the name of the scripture. It was the Bhagavad Gita.

I was surprised by their keen interest in this scripture. I was told, even in Scandinavian countries there was curiosity about Bhagavad Gita. In India, unfortunately the young generation lacks the enthusiasm for this wonderful scripture. How I wish that our young children read and understand this invaluable gift from Sri Krishna.

A verse in the Gita which moves me from within is: Leaves, Flowers, Fruits, I offer to you, my Lord!

Krishna is the God of small things. He loves small gifts. For him small is beautiful, for it epitomizes humility. God does not need the universe; for He Himself has created the Universe. He accepts small things as they are the offerings of a loving heart.

A rich businessman donated Rs. 50000/- for charity. Those Rs. 50000/- are trash if he does not carry love for Krishna; and if he does not bear witness to his teachings. God does not ask us large sums of money. He yearns for true love of our hearts.

A scholar may have read many books. He may be a modern wizard but God does not care for scholarship or for the knowledge. For knowledge without humility is dust. A scholar who has probed into the world of knowledge, but has not cultivated compassion in his heart, is not accepted by the Lord. For books are nothing but dry leaves of knowledge.

For years I searched for a book titled Cosmos. Cosmos contained the description of the infinite Universe. The book has been written by a great scholar. He began to write this book at the age of 76 years and wrote it till he died at the age of 90 years. For 14 years this scholar laboured on the book. Although this book contains scientific information about the Universe and its mystery, it is limited. Now with the advancement of science, it is outdated. What remains, and will continue to remain is the emotion in a man expressed as *Bhakti*, expressed as devotion to the Infinite.

Anything, any quest, which is devoid of love and emotion is sand, it is a desert, dry and wanting. True knowledge, a true quest has to come from deep within. It is loaded with love. What is Love? True love lies in denying oneself the self.

I write :

Move away from personal self: seek rest at his spacious courtyard, abandon all that you posses. You will find the truth, the beautiful one in your heart!

Lose your finite self in the infinite. Then alone will you be one with the Lord, then alone will your limited self-merge with the unlimited self of the Universe.

While in London, I wished to see the British Museum. When I expressed this wish to someone, he replied with a smile that they visited the museum only to see the faces of beautiful girls and not to read the books. They had no love for Knowledge. It is so difficult to find places of knowledge, which are also places of pilgrimage.

One day I go to Wales. The Welsh people are simple, basically not highly educated and not so intellectual. Let me tell you about a brilliant scholar of Welsh county. His English was excellent. Later he became a Member of

Parliament. His oratory was remarkable. He was a man of culture and etiquette. At a Welsh University, discussions and dialogues were common as it believed in promoting the freedom of expression. One day a black man visited the University and we entered into a dialogue at the conference. He requested the permission of the chair to speak a few words. He was the only Blackman at that meeting. He stood up and said with strong conviction, "Oh white men! In the name of justice I impeach you."

I was astounded. The people listened to him in silence. The President of the meeting, a white man got up and nodded.

"This brother from Africa speaks the truth. I shall look into the matter."

I was impressed by the sense of justice of this British.

One fine cloudy day in Wales, I learnt of another great man who had come down from the slopes of mountains. This man was the beloved of many hearts. He came down from the mountains to play music on the violin.

I learnt from the people that they loved to hear him. Music is the food of life, it is said, so play on. I wanted to know more about this man, more about his character and his values. This man's mission in life was to spread joy through music. He did not ask for money. But the people who loved him, sought him and took him for lunch or dinner. I wondered: What is the message this man wants to give?

One of them said, 'He comes to touch our hearts. He moves us to tears.'

I found their love for this violinist extraordinary. I learnt that he was a man of the mountains. He was a simple villager, who spent most part of the year in the mountains playing violin. I also came to know that he loved the poor and spent time with them. A free bird, his soul stirring music enchanted the people. His love for the poor was indeed heart warming. He put his hand in the pocket and took out a coin or two which he passes on to any poor man he meets.

One day this violinist came to the town and saunters into the Bazaar. He saw a beggar who asked for alms. He put his hand in the pocket and searched for a coin, but found none. He felt despondent. Then an idea came to his mind and he invited the beggar to go with him for his lecture in the evening. It was customary in England to put some money in the box after attending the event. On one occasion I also received 10 pounds. On another occasion they collected 15 pounds for me. The musician told the beggar that approximately one thousand people would gather in the evening to listen to his music. And whatever his collection, he would share it with him.

"So please do come with me in the evening," he urges the beggar.

In the evening thousands of people gathered to hear him. He might have collected a large amount of money. He places the whole amount at the feet of the poor beggar and weeps :

"I am sorry. I could not give you anything in the morning. Pray forgive me. Now all the money I have collected, is yours."

After this incident people requested him to speak a few words. His short speech was like a song sung on a flute.

"My dear brothers, my poor folks, all this money has come from you. It belongs to you. I give away all."

May you carry this message: serve the poor like the musician from the mountain of Wales.

This was long ago. Yet, I still dream of him. A musician who played tune to bring joy to this dark sorrow stricken world. A man who lived for others. His teachings, simple though, have penetrated my heart.

In a particular town in England, I was a guest for a few days. My visit was arranged by the Theosophical Society. Annie Besant was its foremost leader. I had already met her in India where she had done a wonderful job of reviving Hinduism. Her disciples in England, had made all the arrangements for me, including organizing meetings in the evening. The meetings were well attended by the English gentry.

At these meetings I was asked many questions. I give you a gist of the question and answer sessions.

Q: The path of Spiritual life is difficult. We live in material world. Is there a way of attaining spirituality under these conditions?

Ans: Reduce your desires. Desires are poison. He who succumbs to desires, creates sorrow for himself. The cause of our unhappiness is our vicarious desires. Be like a lotus which is in the mud, but rises above the muck. Be like a lotus, pure in the world but not of the world.

Be like a lotus : Pour water over the flower, it slips down; it touches the petals but does not remain with it; leaving the lotus pure, fresh and sparkling. So abandon all evil desires. Let sorrow touch you like the water, leaving you glowing bright and beautiful.

Q: What is faith? How to grow in faith? Many unhappy/ tragic incidents in life devastate our faith in God.

Ans: It is true. Faith is often shaken up by unpleasant experiences. Doubts weaken it. Untowardly incidents destroy it.

Q: What should we do?

Ans: Let me tell you a beautiful story that is found in our sacred scriptures. The story runs as :

One day Hazrat Moosa went up to the mountains to pray. Hazrat Moosa was a man of prayer. He says, Oh God I feel so lonely. If you have any friend then kindly send him to me, so that I may feel secure in this insecure world.

The God answers his prayers. Yes I do have a friend, who is known as the friend of the Almighty.

There upon Moosa asks God where to find this friend of the Almighty.

God replies: 'Go up the far mountains and search for him. And you shall find him!'

Hazrat Moosa climbs the mountains. Hardly had he reached there, a terrible stench envelops him. He went closer to the site of stinking stench. He found a man full of wounds. His open sores gave out foul smell. He went closer to him, but seeing his pathetic condition, he said to himself: How can this man punched with sores be the friend of Almighty?

Hazrat Moosa retraced his steps. He turned his back to the man. As he was about to leave, the sick man called out to him and says: Moosa! You came here with great enthusiasm. How is that you are so disappointed and want to go back?

Hazrat Moosa was astonished. How did this man know his name? Was he really the friend of Almighty?

Moosa realized his mistake and got into a conversation with him. You are said to be the friend of Almighty and yet you suffer the pain of these wounds tattooed on your body! You are dear to God, but you are stinking with foul smell. You are a pious devotee of the Lord. Then why does God penalise you with pain?

At this the sick man replied: That is God's way; to give suffering to his devotees; to inflict sorrow upon them. God rejoices in the suffering of his devotees.

Hazrat Moosa was surprised. He said: My dear friend, you are in great pain, in what way can I help you?

The man replied: I have but one desire: to see you. That desire has been duly fulfilled. My second desire is to drink cold water; so kindly get me some cold water to quench my thirst.

Hazrat Moosa immediately ran to get water from a near by well. Excited Moosa called out to the man, as he ran back! I have brought the cold water for you. I have brought the cold water to quench your thirst ! But as he came close to the man, he found him lying flat. He was no more.

Hazrat Moosa was shocked. He prayed to God: Kindly solve this riddle for me. What is the meaning of all this?

This friend of Almighty you had guided me to visit wanted to drink a glass of cold water. I ran and brought him the cold water, but he was dead even before I could reach him. Then again, why do your devotees have to go through this pain and suffering? I am puzzled, Oh Lord! Solve this puzzle for me.

God's reply to Moosa was: My dear Moosa, this devotee of mine had committed two sins for which he had to pay.

1) He suffered from ego, he began to brag about his devotion, his *bhakti*. *Bhakti* has to be silent; devotion has to be concealed within. A true devotee is not vocal about his love for the Lord. How fortunate are those devotees who work silently within. Their relationship with the Lord is kept secret.

2) His second sin was that when he was thirsty, he begged of you to get him some cold water. The true devotee does not seek favours from ordinary human beings. He asks God to provide for his needs. This man should have asked me and I would have provided for his needs. This man should have asked me and I would have provided the cold water to him. But he had no faith in me.

So I say: At the feet of the Lord, ask him whatever you need. At the door of the human beings be a royal King and ask for nothing.

This is the teaching I gave to the people of that town in England: Have faith in God. Whatever the difficulties, whatever the troubles, do not lose heart. But have firm faith in the Almighty. He will take care of all your needs. He will provide you with everything.

Part-II

Lahore Longing

Years ago, I had visited the Shivalik Hills of Shimla. Its cool climate, the snow capped mountains beyond, and the simple hill folks fascinated me. I used to walk miles and miles on the hilly ridges, in the shadow of towering pine trees. I loved the pine scented air, babbling brooks and the rushing streams. These beautiful lyrics of nature touched my heart. The water cascading over the rocky stones and then swirling into a puddle or a pool was a divine prayer for me. Back in Karachi, the scene was totally different. The sea is fascinating in its own way; it reveals its own secrets in its own songs sung by the shore. Besides rivulets and sea, nature hums another tune – The soundless music; the silent music of the soul. No instrument can play this ageless, voiceless song!

In Shimla, I had given a few discourses. Many scholars had attended my lectures. Once a foreigner who had heard my discourse, came up to me and said: "I have great reverence for Sri Ram and the Ramayan and the Bhagavad Gita. But, I feel sorry to say, that I have not found similar devotion in India for these two invaluable scriptures. In Sweden, people respect these volumes of wisdom as sacred world literature." His words saddened my heart.

In Shimla, one day, a few scholars and academicians met together to decide the fate of a college. The institution had inherited a lot of money, and was worth Rs. 40 lakhs. The committee was in search of a suitable person, who would be able to handle this fast growing college. These gentlemen approached me for the post. I declined. They requested me to give it a serious thought. I gave them my home address, before leaving for my home town Hyderabad.

One day, while I was at Hyderabad, I received a telegram from the same college in Lahore. It was an invitation to join the college and accept its headship. This unexpected offer of the post of the principal of the college perplexed me. I had no clue as to who had chosen me for the post. Later, I could figure it out. This was the same post I had been offered in Shimla. Now, for the second time, this opportunity had come my way. I reflected, 'There must be a hidden meaning in what God does'. Perhaps, this was an opportunity given to me to experience Guru Nanak Dev's teachings in the land of his birth. At once, my thoughts rushed to the great prophet of Harmony, and suddenly I felt the need to learn more about him.

Guru Nanak Dev's teachings have fascinated me since my early childhood. I have wept, as I have absorbed his holy words. His teachings stir my heart and wrench it in pain. Perhaps, Lahore had this sublime experience to offer me. I took up this opportunity and started giving discourses on Guru Nanak Dev. Sikhs, Akalis and Khalsas, built huge 'pandals', so as to accommodate crowds who gathered there to listen to me. The crowds were really large: Simple folks, villagers, farm lands and others would travel miles to hear me 'speak' of the Guru. Their love, their yearning, their faith was astounding. They travelled miles and walked about 30 to 45 miles in a faith that is rare in present times. Their feet would be scratched and bruised as they would trudge through the fields and the furrowed earth. They did not mind it at all, for they came for love of the holy word, for love of Guru's *'Bani'*.

It is in Lahore, that I came to know of the great influence Guru Nanak Dev held over that region. I became aware of the presence of this Primordial *Shakti*.

I have travelled far and wide, I have met people from all walks of life, rich and poor, elite and down trodden, affluent and deprived; I have seen palaces and humble huts, I have seen the urban sophistication and the rural simplicity. I have visited citadels of power and parliaments. I have met saints, sages, sinners and criminals; I have met young and the old, but it is the holy men, the saints who revere and seek their blessings.

I had many esoteric experiences in Lahore. But I shall speak only of one. There was this *Fakir*, his name was Hassan. He was a true mystic, always immersed in ecstasy of his being. He was called 'Lal Hassan'. The red one; for he was swathed in the red colour of love. Hassan was a true spiritualist. He saw oneness in all. He had a secularist vision of life – Hindus, Muslims, birds and beasts were all images of that One Being. His love was universal and unconditional; spirituality knows no caste, no creed, and no boundaries. In His eyes all are one.

Let me tell you about Hassan. Once, he went to the market place. A small Hindu boy was selling *'Chole'* (cooked chick peas). Hassan saw the boy and uttered, 'How gentle, how sweet is he,' saying so he embraced the boy with love and affection. 'How fortunate, how blessed am I to meet such a one'. His joy knew no bounds. Hassan had seen God's image in the innocence of the *Chole* vendor.

Recollecting this incident I am reminded of another Sufi mystic, a spiritual maverick who was also caught by the innocent charm of a small boy. His name is Bekas. Like Bekas, Hassan too went into a trance at the sight of this Hindu boy selling *Chole* in the market place.

Love has spread its splendour,
for colourless Hassan is dipped, in the red Wine love of.

Even the Sindhi Sufi Mystic said so:

'I have seen the Loved one, I have seen His wonder. My Beloved, my dear one, my dream, my desire, my love, I have seen all this in the pure innocence of that boy selling things in the market place, I have seen colours in the colourless one. I have seen the vibrant colours of the spring, colours of the joy in that human being. God became manifest in that beautiful innocent human form.' Enthralled by that Divinity, the Sindhi *Fakir* wished to be one with the Lord.

Even Hassan *Fakir* exclaimed, Ah – you are still far from me!

This *fakir* of our beloved Sind, said again and again:
I am sold out again. I am sold out to you, my beloved. Even before

I was born, I have been sold out to you. I was yours, oh Mehboob. Open the Divine door and let me in.

This *Fakir* Hassan of Lahore lived in the similar ecstasy of yearning. To this day his anniversary is celebrated in Shalimar Gardens, Lahore. Thousands of devotees gather to pay their humble homage to Hassan *Fakir*.

My dear fellow devotees please remember one thing. This Hassan Fakir sings soul stirring Kafis* – in Punjabi, which are sung even today in rural Punjab by the village folk. One Kafi is:
All my friends are noble and virtuous – I am full of faults!
I am a trespasser; help me to cross this ocean of filth.
I am a sinner, I am guilty-Pardon my faults,
Forgive me, and guide me to the shinning shore.

What is true service? The one who serves the *Sangat* and the *Pangat;* one who respects others and serves them in utter humility is better than him, who thinks himself to be a lowly servant of God.

Many who serve, alas! Go astray, wandering in the dark Maya of greed and power. Serve not like them, imposing views and authority on others. Serve as serveth the plate. Sing on the flute of thy heart! Sing it so that others too, may sing with thee! Sing and Serve.

Everyone has dyed the wedding garment in splendid colours;
Now it is my turn to dye my garment in the splendour of Name Divine!
Who is my Beloved? asks the same Fakir. Who is my soul-mate?

---

* 'Kafi' is a souful devotional song

Where is my home? My Beloved, my companion, my soul-mate is He, the Lord !
I have jumped into the river, while I carry a heavy burden on my head !

The burden of misdeeds, evil thoughts, and the many sins of this world, is breaking me. How may I cross the turbulent river? Rescue me O Lord, and help me swim through the stormy waters of this world.

"All my life, I have wandered in 'the hills', in fun and frolics of the trivial world," says Hassan, "Death hangs above my head, Lord, I repose faith in thee. Ferry me safely across, ferry me to your divinity. O Merciful one, Forgive my sins, I have lost the battle. Now I need thee and thee alone."

May this aspiration of Hassan Fakir, touch your heart and may you cry out:
Ferry me across these dark waters, my Lord,
I am a sinner, save me, Lest, I drown and die.

In Lahore, the early morning cold of winter kept people indoors. But I used to go out for a walk in the Big Garden. There were very few fellow walkers. The cold kept them indoor. I could align myself with the Nature, and communicate to it my deepest feelings of heart. I would cry out to God and would invoke Divine grace thus:

O my Lord, I am full of faults
Give me, a glance of grace,
Ferry me, through the stormy waters
To the safety of your shore.

In Lahore, a foreigner wearing Indian *'Desi'* clothes came to visit me.

'From where do you come, sir?' I asked.
'From Holland'. He replied.
'What brings you to India?'

'A book called Gita. Years ago, I read it. It captivated my heart, I felt a strange pull to the country of its origin. I am a pilgrim here.'

'Your reverence for Gita is astonishing. Does the west also feel the same way about this sacred scripture?'

'People in the west respect India because of this scripture,' he replied.

A few days later, I met another person in the same place.

He was a Muslim scholar. Naturally we entered into a spiritual cum intellectual dialogue. What he said took me by surprise.

'The spiritual literature of the Prophet (peace be on earth) in Arabic is incomplete. We need to include one more sacred book,' he said.

'What book?' I asked in all humility.

'Bhagavad Gita', he replied without hesitation, 'I have great reverence for that sacred book. I have translated it into Arabic, so that my Muslim brothers and sisters can read it.'

Lahore would get very cold in winter, so cold that I could not bear it. My friends advised me, that I should take a morning stroll, in order to keep my body warm. Taking their suggestion I started going out for a walk at

6 am in the morning, even though it would be freezing cold. Again at around 12 noon, I would go out for a stroll enjoying the warmth of the winter sun.

During one of my morning walks, I once met a learned scholar, a High Court judge. He had received his higher education in England but had great love for Indian ideals and Hindu scriptures. He was Justice Shade Lal. We got along well and hence made it convenient to meet at a common point and then walk together, to the open garden. The warmth of his company kept the cold away.

On one such cold wintry morning, I went to the Garden, all alone. I walked through its leafy trees, drinking the silence of Nature, exulting in its beauty. The Garden had hundreds of huge trees. But one tree stood out in its green majesty. I was struck by its beauty. I gazed at it: wondering what made the tree so special and so unique. Can you guess? Sitting under the canopy of this tree was a *Fakir*; his gaze was fixed; his eyes were intoxicated and blazing, his body was meditative and still, in that shivering cold of the early morning of Lahore winter! Absolutely absorbed in Divine ecstasy, he exuberated serenity of a rare kind. His eyes were like, a flame burning. He was lost in an experience, invisible to us. He was in a blissful state of divine ecstasy.

I humbly bowed down to this man of God. He gestured to me to sit down, and I sat by his side in silence. In silence I marvelled at his 'fixed' gaze; in silence I observed his blissful state. He was in a heavenly sphere. He was lost to Divine ecstasy. He appeared to be in a trance but he was fully awake.

After a while, he got up, came close to me, and smiled, radiating a light which is difficult to describe in words. With a mop of curly hair and wearing light clothing his bright eyes lit by inner flame, he smiled again. That smile was magical, it touched my soul. He hugged me and folded me in his embrace. Blessed was I to taste that love; blessed was I to have the privilege of meeting such a Divine soul.

We sat in silence, gazing at each other. Words failed, dialogue would be meaningless, and the spell of spiritual silence was absolute, vibrating and radiating love; peace and divinity. In that ecstatic mood, tears welled up in my eyes. I was overwhelmed by his soulful gaze – gaze which was like a burning flame, that was illuminating in itself – it purified me. It purified my body, mind and the spirit. I was fortunate to meet him, sit by him, and be clasped in the embrace of his love. What he said thrilled me to no end. "These tears of yearning in your eyes, will take you across to the golden shore. These tears are your true treasure!"

Through out that day, these words echoed within me. They kept ringing in my heart. *These tears are your true treasure*.

I would like to keep before you my fellow devotees this one thought: Tears of longing are a rich treasure, a rare gift which you can really offer to the Lord in humility and love.

There was a time when I used to walk miles and miles. I used to walk briskly. But now God in his kindness and mercy has made me immobile. I am unable to walk.

I recollect an incident here that took place in Lahore in Punjab. I was in the habit of waking up early. I would get up at pre dawn hour of four 0'clock, and do my morning chores. Covered in warm clothes, I would go out for a walk even though it would be dark and bitter cold outside. I would shiver in the biting cold; still I would continue to walk miles and miles. One early morning as usual I left for the Big garden. I kept on walking miles and miles. Tired at last, I looked around for a way to return home. "Where is my home?" I asked a few passers by. They burst out laughing. "your home? you should be knowing about your home. How would we know where is your home?" They ridiculed me.

True enough, how would those passers by know, where my home was? Where was it? Where was my home? Physically exhausted, I looked around for signs of a return path. I hailed simple village folks going to work. "Tell me," I urged them, "Where is my home?" They were surprised. They asked for a landmark, or a sign near the house.

"I stay next to the famous professor of mathematics who works in the university. He has a first class degree from the Cambridge University. He is a renowned scholar and lives in a large bungalow with a huge compound. My residence is next to his." The villagers were puzzled. "What do we know of a professor? We are simple village folks," they replied innocently.

Where is my home? the question rattles again and again. Exhausted, and unable to figure out my existing location, I lie down under the shade of a tall and well spread out tree. My whole body was stiff from pain. I kept wondering; 'Where is my home? Where is my home?' The passers by seemed curious and puzzled. At last after several queries and with the help of many people I was able to find the road leading to my house. By this time, tiredness and fatigue had overtaken me. I stepped into a house and requested its people to allow me to rest for a while, acquianting them with the fact that I had lost my way, and I still had a long way to go. They readily agreed. After taking some rest, I ventured out in the garden and sat down. By now, the evening dusk had set in. A few people walked up to me. I enquired from them whether they knew where my home was! Someone in that motley crowd asked me my name. "I am Vaswani," I replied.

"We know you. We have heard you. We know where you live." They took me home. As I walked with them towards my home, I remembered a verse from Bhagvat Gita. 'O Arjuna! Come, come, unto Me! Seek refuge in Me for your abode is at My feet!'

Our true home is as pure and gentle as breeze. Our true abode is an illuminated sphere of light. It can be found only at the blessed feet of Lord Krishna.

Our worldly homes are full of conflicts. There are clashes of personalities and conflicts of interests. There is turmoil and there is vice and virtue, there is prayer and punishment. Opposite forces, love and hate, create chasm and disintegration in the family. Absorbed in mundane thoughts of daily existence, we become obsessed with the 'self'. Our nights are dark, and our mornings are filled with hazy thoughts. Happiness? Bliss? True happiness is found in our true home! Our real home, our true abode is at the feet of Shyam Sunder, our Beloved Sri Krishna.

In Lahore, for a while I was a guest in the house of a rich man. He owned a shoe factory and was doing very well in his business. He was honest, truthful and religious. His wife too was a devotee of the Lord. The early morning prayer in their house was heavenly. After lighting the *Havan Kund*, they recited the sacred scriptures. The blend of prayer and puja created a beautiful environment. I always joined the family in this ritual of puja after I returned from the early morning walk.

The dancing flames in the *Havan kund* fascinated me. The large quantities of ghee and sugar made the tongues of flames to rise high, creating an aura which was both mystical and magical.

I experienced many mystical and strange happenings on my early morning walks. I normally took lonely and abandoned paths, so as to avoid meeting people. Once in a while, I would cross a hut, and its watch dog would bark, follow me some distance and then go back quietly. Whenever I felt tired, I sat by the trees, experiencing the abundance of Nature, and enjoying the sounds of silence. In that silence, I often thought of Lord Krishna, how with his benevolent glance of grace, he would touch the hearts of criminals and sinners and transform them into better human beings.

One day, reflecting on the teachings of Gita, I say to myself, 'It is not necessary, that to prove my devotion to the Lord, I have to physically go and serve the poor and the forsaken. I can serve the Lord, by spending time with the little ones, and be blessed by them.' I make a deep study of The Gita.

The more I reflect on the teachings of Gita, the more pronounced is the voice within, 'Be the Guardian of the weak and the forsaken and serve the lowly and the poor. Be in the company of the little ones, and be blessed.

Therefore, the first principle of my life is, be of service to poor and the broken ones.

Sunday was observed as a day of silence. Although I was the Principal of a College, I cooked my own food on Sundays. I would eat one meal of dal, rice and potatoes. The rest of the day was spent in silent meditation. The doors of the house would be closed with the instructions not to allow any one in. This was my *sadhana* discipline.

Then, it so happened, that one day, my inner voice said, "Oh Lord, shower me thy grace.

Slate the thirst of this bird

With the waters of thy Divine Mercy."

My favourite prayer has been 'O Sai, forgive me every time I go astray,

Shower me with the waters of thy spirit, so that I may be cleansed and do not go astray.'

When I was the Principal of Dayal Singh College, I had many servants. Nevertheless, every morning, I bowed down to my mother and touched her feet "Bless me mother", I would whisper. To this she would reply, "Son, you are already blessed !" My mother had come to stay with me for a few months. This gave me a golden opportunity to serve her and seek her blessings.

One evening, when I returned home, my mother said, "Son, the straps of the cot have become loose. Call one of your servants to tighten them."

I myself took up the task of tightening the straps.

My mother was upset, "Son, you have so many servants around, why don't you ask them to do this."

"Mother," I replied, "Am I not your servant?"

My eyes were filled with tears. I had served my mother well and in return earned her rich blessings.

I ask of you this my dear fellow devotees, serve your mother and earn her blessings. Remember mother is your first Guru.

While, I was the Principal of Dayal Singh College, Lahore, Sir Jagdish Chander Bose was invited there to give lecturers at the university. We were all excited to meet this genius of India. He was to be accompanied by his wife. This news spread like wild fire. Speculation about Lady Bose ran high. People wondered how gracious, fashionable and sophisticated would Lady Bose be.

When Sir Jagdish Chandra Bose arrived in the hall, all eyes were attentive. People craned their necks to have a look at Lady Bose. For there was none with him who could fit into the image of the titled lady. The woman accompanying him was a very simple person. She was wearing a white khadi sari. To every one's astonishment she was Lady Bose. How simple ! exclaimed the audience. Indeed, we were taken aback, struck by her utter simplicity.

Even though she was highly educated, and came from a renowned family of royal standing, her simplicity and humility was an example for all of us to follow.

Lal Loi, a mid-winter festival of north India, is celebrated with great enthusiasm by the young and the old alike. My Punjabi students, many of whom were Sikh boys, also celebrated Lal Loi with great fervour. On that particular Lal Loi day, it was icy cold. My students had organized the festival and requested me to be present for the event.

In that bitter cold, we sat around the logs of burning wood. Large tongues of flame leaped into the air. Scarlet red, burning bright flames wove dazzling patterns of light, bewitchingly beautiful, and amusing me to no end. Caught by the enticing dance of fire, I gazed at the magic of the sparkling illumination and reflected:

Fire is fascinating. It keeps away the cold. Fire is illuminating. It burns away the evil. Fire is red, scarlet red, reminding us of nobility of love, that burns itself to sacrifice for others.

The night of Lal Loi was spent in prayers and recitation of *Gurbani*. May we understand the implicit meaning of this festival. Every festival is a celebration of profound thought. It brings us in rhythm with the cycle of Nature.

The red flame burning, is the symbol of true unconditional love.

The divisive forces disintegrating our nation, are rooted in narrow selfish regionalism. Sind has been separated, Sindhis have been alienated, and Sindhis need the warmth of Lal Loi. Punjab has been mutilated. Punjabis need the comfort of the mystical flames of Lal Loi. Bengal is bifurcated – Bengalis need the brightness of sacred fire of Lal Loi.

Today, I reflect upon the symbolic significance of Lal Loi. I invoke God's blessings and pray. Ignite the fire, tend the flames, and burn the sparklers of love, love which is universal, sacrificing and selfless.

> My heart is a flame.
> The fires of longing raging my heart.
> Come, Oh Beloved, slate my thirst,
> I am burning, like Lal Loi,
> Come, Oh Beloved, with the waters of the spirit;
> Teach me, to love, all mankind :
> Poor and rich, old and young,
> Broken and bleeding,
> Come, Oh Beloved, together we sing
> The song of Lal Loi, the fire is raging...
> And embrace the world in Love Divine.

The true meaning of Lal Loi is LOVE- love for the Great Masters, love for the Guru, love for the fellow devotees and love for fellow human beings. Love which embraces the universe.

Ecstasy of Mystics

My mother passed away on the sacred day of 'Akhandteej'. It was my deep desire, that God should give me an opportunity to serve my mother. At that point of time, I was working away from home. As soon as I received the telegram of my mother's illness, I immediately rushed to Karachi. God had provided an opportunity to serve my mother when she was on her death bed. I was thankful to God for that. My mother blessed me profusely. Let me share a secret with you. Whatever I am today is due to the blessings of my parents. I had a chance to serve my father, when his end was coming near. I had the same opportunity, when my mother was about to shed her physical form. God has been abundantly kind in granting me this boon of serving my parents during the last days of their journey on this earth. Night after night, I sat by my mother's bed side and received her blessings. During this period, I came to know of my mother's true nature. Recalling that moment of my mother's death, I am reminded of the words:

A devotee's face glows with purity,
For hidden behind that veil, is a radiant soul!

These are the words of a *fakir* saint. A true devotee's pure soul is concealed behind a veil. Nevertheless, the beauty of the soul shows on the face. I saw this beautiful glow on my mother's face, hours before she was to drop her physical form. Her true self, her beauteous self became manifest and spread a magical glow on her face. That picture of illuminated face is difficult for me to forget. Such an illumination comes from the recitation of the Holy name. My mother was linked with the Infinite. Just before she breathed her last, I asked her a question that had been bothering me for some time. "Dear mother, now that you are embarking on another journey, how do you feel? Do you think I have been a nuisance to you? Have I disobeyed you? Have I displeased you? Many a times you have asked me to get married, and I have flatly refused. That may have hurt you. I know that you prayed, and fasted, so that I may come around and accept your proposal to get married. I know I have disobeyed you on that one count. Now tell me, my dear mother, how do you feel about me?"

She smiled and pinched my cheek with affection. "My dear son, I am very happy. I leave this world as a fully contented person. It is good that you did not marry. I don't have any regrets, for you have been a good son in every sense of the term. You have sent me your entire salary every month. You have looked after me very well. I am very happy indeed."

Her words relieved me. I felt relaxed. A heavy burden had been lifted off my chest. My mother indeed was a true devotee of the Lord. Today as ever, I seek her blessings as I bow down to her sacred memory. As soon as my mother began to sink, we began chanting the Holy Name. The chanting and the recitation continued all night till ten in the morning, even after we had returned from the cremation ground. The holy sounds filled the air like an aroma of joss sticks burning in the room. The environment was peaceful and blissful.

It is difficult to describe my love for my mother. My love for her was like a vast sea; love which only she or God could fathom. Yet, I did not shed a tear when she passed away. I requested my family members not to weep; not to mourn the death of the dear one. Even today, my love for my mother is fathomless. I continue to seek her blessings every moment of my life.

The night my mother passed away, I resigned from my job as the Principal of Mahindra College, Patiala. That night I prayed, "God grant me the strength to renounce the world and be a true *fakir*." I think, I am still far from that ideal. Yes, true renunciation means absence of worldly thoughts of ambition, of power, of position and of authority. A true '*fakir*' is a beggar, who is devoid of all pride and ego. When I gave up my principal's post of a college, I reiterated to myself that I should be egoless; that I would be a beggar, and would beg like an ascetic, without the feeling of shame, of hurt or dejection. It was difficult for a shy person like me to beg at someone's door. But to be a true *fakir*, I had to adhere to my resolve.

I moved away to another town. I decided that from the next day onwards, I would go out and beg for food. I woke up early, took my bath and ventured out on this difficult task of 'begging'. Doubts assailed me but only for a moment. How would you beg? The proud face of ego jibbed at me. But God gave me the strength to try out my *'fakiri'*, - my egoless existence. I walked around and I came upto a friend's house. Should I tell him, that I have come to beg at your door? I hesitated but rebuked myself. *Learn to be humble*. Learn to beg! I pluck up enough courage to say to my friend: 'I have come to beg'.

'You are welcome,' he replied warmly. 'It is my good fortune that you have come to my door.'

At that moment, I realised that things which seemingly appear to be difficult were indeed not so difficult to achieve. May be, God was being kind to me. On this journey of life, temptations abound. Vices lead you astray. By the Grace of God, I have overcome many weaknesses with the prayer:

'Merciful One.
Shower mercy on this sinner.'

Of Fakirs And Fakiri

A time comes in my life when I realise the truth of my being. The purpose of my life becomes clear. It is to grow in spirit : to cultivate the soul and reach for the limitless sky. Then the question arose in my mind : How to cultivate the soul?

The one answer I receive is : *the world is full of distractions. Be detached. Every thing is effervescent. Therefore tend the Eternal flame*: Cultivate the soul in silence. It was during this time in my life, that I began to comprehend and to enjoy the spiritual writings of the Great Ones. I developed a liking for that great Sindhi poet, Shah Abdul Latif. His poetry is lyrical, melodious, mystical and spiritual. It is pragmatic as it is rich with the wisdom of Vedanta. It is a love wine that takes you to the heady heights of Sufism. I began to study Shah Abdul Latif. His poetry has a rare spiritual quality as seen in the following verse:

> Awake O fool. Give up your laziness.
> Awake to the Truth. Why do you scramble
> For enticing shadows of nothingness?

Why run after material 'shadows'? What will you gain in this rat race? Awake. Don't be entangled in these cobwebs; know well that they will disappear like a cloud under the sun. I take my first step on the spiritual path with the help of the above *mantra*. Awake! Arise!

In the beginning I thought it would be an easy task. But it proved to be a tough one.

What does Shah say further?

> *'In silence they climbed,*
> *Unheard,*
> *In silence they scaled the mountain peak.'*

I began to understand the deeper meaning of these verses. The soul can be cultivated only in silence. 'Grow in silence'. Further Shah hails:

> *In silence they sailed and reached the shore (of Porbunder).*
> *Open your eyes. Do not fall a slumber.*
> *Be away from the muck of this world,*
> *Lest you may scream, waking to a nightmare.*

To avoid the nightmare of this world, I escaped to my small place. I practised silence ... . Except for an hour's stroll, I was confined to a small space. I was by myself, learning to be still in silence. Because Shah says those who remain in silence reach the peak. I became obsessed with the awareness, that silence was not only golden; it was an invaluable aid to spiritual growth. Silence became a habit with me.

Close to this village where I lived was a small town which had a post office savings bank. Every month I travelled there to withdraw Rs.10/- – rupees ten – for my monthly expenses. That small amount of rupees ten was sufficient to see me through a month.

One day, I met an old friend at the P.O.S. bank. He was surprised to see me, and wondered what was wrong with me. 'Look at your clothes. They are soiled. Your hair is crusted with dust. You have not even combed your hair.' He conveyed a sense of shock, eyeing me from head to toe. What answer could I give him?

'Look at your condition!' he said with deep concern, 'what have you been doing to yourself?' he asked bewildered.

'I have been in the service of my Lord. He has taken such good care of me. He has safeguarded all my interests. He is the one who has protected me. In His service, I remain.'

This long lost friend was astonished. He saw my 'unkept' clothes and tousled hair, and wonders some madness has gone into me. How do I tell him, that He has really taken care of me, by putting me in the company of *Fakirs*. Believe me, *Fakirs* are true friends. They never forsake you! It is in their company that I search for a secret route, that by-passes the noisy *bazaar* called world! I wanted to eschew the harsh din of the *bazaar*, lest I turned deaf to the Reality, and miss the Truth I was looking for!

Around that time, Khilafat conference took place in this very town. Delegates from all over the country had poured in. People were ready to quarrel and strike back with guns. There were discordant notes every where, the echoes of which had reached my room and rippled the silence within my being. I yearned to go to this *Fakir*, and learn from him, the Art of Silence, so that I could reach Porbunder safely! The *Fakir* was aware of the social and political climate of the country, was even aware of the divergent groups which had descended on this town; and he too had heard the discordant notes of bigotry. But he was calm. He gave me the teachings in two lines,

> Step aside of the procession,
> Feel the thirst for the shore!

What does that mean? Gradually, I began to grasp its core meaning. Leave all that was happening around you; concentrate on your own goal; the goal of spiritual development!

I asked the *Fakir* again – How to be outside the mainstream of life and be focused on the goal?

The *Fakir* quoted from Bedil. He gave me the message. Bedil sings:

> Go through this life unseen,
>   Hide within the Hidden One!

I searched for a true *Fakir*, who would help me to 'grow in silence'. God is Invisible, we should go through this life, as the 'invisible'. Lose our own identity and merge with the Invisible. It is a simple verse; but its meaning is very deep! The world is full of strife. Life is filled with disappointments and frustrations. It is this suffering that will erase the ego and take away pride; it will grind, till you vanish into thin air.

How will you vanish into obscurity? By avoiding both the good and the bad; by forsaking both the virtues and the vices. Even the Bhagavad Gita urges : O Arjuna, be away from fame and notoriety.

Man is a thinking animal. He has the power of discretion. If you wish to ascent the spiritual path, then be away from life's superficialities. Devote yourself to the silent work of life.

Do not tangle yourself with the rituals and ceremonies of religion. These religious fads take you away from the reality of spirituality. One brother comes to me and puts a large dot of *'tilak'* on my head. Oh, dear devotee, this is an external and rather superficial expression of religion. Go within. Go deep! Even the beads of rosary are an empty chanting, if your mind, heart and soul are not tuned to the Lord!

Once you are free of rituals and ceremonies, the external expressions of religion, you will drink the wine of Love Divine. Get high on that wine and remain in that ecstasy.

Take the instance of Sri Chaitanaya Mahaprabhu. Drunk on the Divine Love, he went into the ecstasy of *'Hari Bol, Hari Bol Bhai!'* People mocked at him, 'this great scholar, who taught great many students is now obsessed with the chant of *Hari Bol*. A professor dancing on the road with *Hari Bol*? Tell me, how would people understand the Divine madness, the Divine obsession, the Divine Love that had possessed him? Can an ordinary person understand the extra-ordinary? So if you are on the spiritual path, quit these mundane pursuits. Quit the craze for living; instead acquire the zest for the Truth, which will put you on the right path.

Life is not a *quid pro quo*. It is when you rise above this that you will be swept away by the storm of love, and be drowned in its boundless ecstasy. It is this storm of positive energy which will ultimately raise you to the Invisible power force called God. This experience of bliss, this ecstasy is indeed beyond description. It has no boundary, no outline. Bedil also sings so :

You are the same, you are the One,
Then why this shyness, why this veil?

Aren't you a part of the Invisible? Then give up all your inhibitions; give up all your veils. Just merge into the ecstasy and enjoy the bliss of being one with him.

You Are An Unlimited Energy

Once I suggested to a *Satsangi* devotee that 'we should dance when we sing.' His reaction was brusque. 'How can we dance when the *Kirtan* is on?' He asked aghast. I would humbly request you : Leave all your inhibitions. In this Love Divine, there are neither the boundaries nor the borders. Neither the veils, nor the '*burquas*'. Neither the walls nor the webs. Get intoxicated on the Love Divine, and bear witness to Shyam Sunder!

Who are you? You are the Light.
Who are you? You are the Radiance.

Who are you? You are the Flame.
Who are you? You are the Light of Heavens.

Why should you be barbed by inhibitions? Why don't you bear witness to God who is limitless, without any fence, and without boundary?

You are the image of God. You are his reflection. You are His light. Then why hide behind the mask? Why hide yourself behind a veil? O' Man, realize : you are a limitless energy; you are Infinite Light. Only if you, my dear *satsang* devotees, would realize, you would know the power that lies within you. Even if you realize an atom of that energy, even if you strike a spark of that divinity, you would be a changed person. Know thy true self, thy potential, thy reality and the Truth. There is no need to read books or scriptures. All you have to do is to go within.

The question often asked is : How to go within?

Two things are necessary for that. Silence and Meditation.

Hence the call of the Fakir who said :
Remove the veil of ignorance and go within.
Awake from those dreams;
Abandon those desires,
Look within and behold the Reality ;
Awake from those dreams,
Abandon those desires,
Look within. Behold the Reality.
Remove the veil of ignorance
And go within!
Forget the bookish teachings. For He is within.

While I reflect upon this one thought, I feel the need to integrate my scattered life. I feel to bind myself to the Lord! How? In what way am I to integrate and build my life? It is then that I lay down three disciplines-sadhanas-for myself.

The first discipline : Live in silence. Be away from the din and drone of this world. Build your life in silence.

At that time I was living in a small town. A few sisters and brothers had collected money and gave it to me. It totalled up to rupees three thousand. I handed over the money back to them with the words : Build a hall where men and women can sit in silence and meditate.

The municipality of that town granted them a free plot of land to build the hall for meditation. I further requested them to build a small wash room with a water tap inside the place. The house I lived in, did not have a water tap. If the hall had a wash room I could bathe in there. Till now I bathed and washed my clothes under the tap in the open. I prayed to Lord, that I may continue this life of simplicity.

The second discipline: Root your life in simplicity. What is a life of simplicity? I made certain rules for myself. One of the rules was, that I should wash my own clothes.

The third discipline : *Naam – simran*. I made it a habit to pick up a word or a phrase from the sacred scriptures and recite it continuously. *"Tum Thakur, tum pe ardaasa,"* is a phrase I love to recite. I also used to recite verses from Shah Abdul Latif and other Sufi saints. In this third discipline of *naam kirtan*, many amazing things happened. I received many insights into the Invisible world. I hoped *Naam Kirtan* would show me the light, and will illuminate the path of spirituality. I often rebuked myself. Awake. Get out of this slumber. Time and again I have quoted Shah Abdul Latif's saying, *those who live in silence, ascend the peak.*

Intoxicated Sufis

I love the company of *Fakirs*, Sages and Saints. One day I went to visit a *Fakir*. I humbly begged of this *Fakir* to enlighten me. "It is said that in silence you reach the peak, in silence you traverse the road, in silence you sail smoothly and reach the shore. Pray, tell me, the nature of this silence. Teach me the technique of this silence that will carry me to the yon golden shore."

The *Fakir* replied to me in a song. The song belongs to Bedil.

Till then, I was unaware of Bedil's Sufism. With the passage of time I began to understand him and appreciate his philosophy. He was a noble soul. Sind was indeed fortunate to be blessed by this great one!

Perhaps few of you know that Sind has a sacred town on the right bank of river Sindhu. It is called Rohri. The blessed Rohri was the hub of many spiritual seekers. I loved this shrine of spirituality. How I wish I could go to Pakistan and visit this holy place once again.

In reverence, I call this holy place as Rohri Sharif. I often reminiscence about Rohri and its great souls. Rohri was the seat of '*mast fakirs*', mystics lost in the ecstasy of the Divine intoxicated by the spiritual wine. Our scriptures refer to these souls as *'Avdhoot'*. Rohri was vibrant with the magic of *pirs, fakirs,* saints and *Sufis,* *'Avdhoots'*.

Bedil too lived there. He was referred to as *'Barra Sai'*; the older *Sai* had a son, who was equally intoxicated with the love of the Lord – Bekas - who was called the *'younger Sai'*. Bedil's anniversary was celebrated with great aplomb and devotion. Many of his disciples came from far and near, to receive the blessings of this *sufi darvesh*.

In Rohri I heard many devotional hymns. I remembered. It was a cold wintry night. A spiritual festival was on. I wished to spend the night there. I carried a small bed roll. The night vigil when devotees expressed gratitude, seeking the blessings and invoking the benediction of the *'Mursheeds'* was touching. People thronged this place, and kept awake the whole night to receive the holy vibrations. Amidst all these prayers, a *fakir* sang on *Ektara* a mystic sufi song. I was fortunate to see 'that' *fakir*, hear him and take his blessings. It was a moving saga of devotion and *bhakti* at the *dargah* of Bedil. Rohri is sacred. Rohri is a place of pilgrimage. Bedil was an extra-ordinary man. His third eye was open. Physically his foot was twisted. But his spiritual ascendancy was very high. He would sit on a small string cot, his face glowing with strange radiance. In his own words, he was a 'lame beggar', but in my opinion he was the pride of Rohri.

Bedil lived an austere life, eating whatever food was brought to him. His love and his spiritual insight were vast. On one occasion, a devotee brought to him one *'chapati'*. Eight Fakirs were sitting by him. 'Let's divide this *chapati* into nine pieces. Let's share it!' Imagine the mystic's greatness and his love for the poor. Whatever money people gave him, he gave it away all to the poor. Bedil was a poet who served the downtrodden in utmost humility. He was a picture of simplicity. A few devotees lived with him. But he did not allow them to do his 'personal' chores. He washed his own clothes and lived a hidden life in his small room.

Pilgrimage To Patna

At this juncture, I recall my stay in Patna. A devotee of the Lord came to visit me. He was an extremely simple man. Who was he? He was 'Rajendra Prasad'. A political stalwart, he was a man of utter humility. Later he became the President of India. He visited me in my room and we had a meaningful dialogue. I will not go into the details of it except that this man, Rajendra Prasad, was a son of the soil. He was down to earth and very humble.

In Patna I was asked a question. What brings you to Patna? I replied: I have come as a pilgrim. My visit to Patna is a pilgrimage. Patna to me is sacred. Do you know, who asked me that question? The father of Dr. B. C. Roy, who later became the Chief Minister of Bengal. He was a great scholar and a giant among intellectuals. He took great care of me while I was in London. It was said at that time, that he was India's best doctor. Whenever Mahatma Gandhi fell ill, this doctor would rush from Calcutta to treat him. He was a man of high ideals and noble virtues. He rightly deserved to be the Chief Minister of Bengal. His father, a well known doctor, lived in Patna. It was he who asked me, what brings you to Patna?

'I am on a pilgrimage.'

'What kind of a pilgrimage is this for a person like you?'

'A very rare pilgrimage. This house is sacred for me. For this is the house, where my dear Guru, my beloved teacher, darling of Sindhis, Sadhu Hiranand passed away. Your house is sacred. It is a place of pilgrimage. It is truly blessed.'

Hearing this Dr. Roy narrates anecdotes from the life of Sadhu Hiranand. Sadhu Hiranand may not have been famous, but he was a divine soul.

Justice Gurudas Bannerjee

In Patna, I met another noble soul. He was the brother of Chittranjan Das. He was a barrister and later became the Judge of Patna High Court. He was full of love for Sri Krishna. In spite of holding a high post, his devotion for Lord Krishna was amazing. His *'Bhakti'* for Shyam Sunder, transcended his knowledge and scholarship. He had lived in England for a while. Nevertheless, he remained rooted in the *bhakti* of Lord Krishna. On the auspicious day of Janmashtami, he delivered a lecture on 'Lord Krishna'. Thousands of people had gathered to hear him. People respected him; loved him. I too yearned to sit at his feet, and listen to his holy words.

Bengalis are emotional people. A Bengali heart is full of *Bhakti*, something which I appreciate and respect.

Justice Gurdas Bannerjee was a judge of Calcutta High Court. In those days, he drew a salary of Rs. 4000/ and more. Yet, this judge of High Court gave spiritual discourses to people and they fondly heard him. An intellectual of a high order, he attracted people from all walks of life. He lived a simple life. Today, we find men holding high positions, flaunting their wealth and scholarship, much in variance to our ideals of Rishi Culture.

Whenever I heard Justice Gurdas Bannerjee I shed tears. I was asked why I shed tears. What did I reply? "He has the wisdom of a *Rishi*? To you he is a Justice of High Court – to me he is a true *Rishi*. He had special love for his mother. He did not enjoy holidays – but spent his vacations with his mother. His mother did not know English, nevertheless he loved her and always encouraged others to care for their mothers, and to serve them. Bengal of those days had produced many such great men; a rare breed who combined scholarship with utmost devotion; for this reason Bengal was the Pride of India. Bengal was in the vanguard of the socio-cultural political rejuvenation of India. The devotion of Justice Gurdas Bannerjee left an indelible mark on my life."

There was a time, when Janmashtami was celebrated with great enthusiasm, love and reverence. But now? Those who are in the high posts and enjoy the lime light, have forgotten their spiritual heritage. Do not be like them. Be humble and listen to the Call of Gita. Imbibe its message and spread it till it echoes in the far off lands.

Spiritual Light

I have had the privilege to see spiritual light shining among the poor, the villagers and the farmers. Once I was invited to a village to give a discourse. Many came to listen; many came from far off villages; poor and lowly folks; they would sit, singing songs, fully immersed in devotion. I learnt great many things from these village folks. One day, a villager comes with *Ek Tara*, and asked whether I would like to hear his song. I requested for a song which wafts the sweet fragrance of the Spirit. Away from the noise and din of city, I longed for devotional music which would seep into my soul. This villager was lost in himself. Then he said: 'Listen. I spend the night in silence. I ask the Lord, *Satguru*, thou art All! Do tell me, who art Thou? Then I sing this song :

Ram simmer, Ram simmer
Yehi Tero karj hai.

(sing the name of the Lord, sing, this is your path)

With tearful eyes he sang for a while. Tears trickled down his cheeks. I too wept. Looking at the pink flowers on the table, he asked innocently, 'May I have them?' I wondered for a moment, what was it that he wants? Pointing to flowers, he said, 'I want these pink flowers'. Tenderly he picked up the flowers, and kissed them profusely uttering, 'O Beloved, O my love'. I was wonder struck; my urban mind was humbled by the sweet gesture of this simple folk singer. We both sat in silence. After a while, he bid me farewell. 'This is the true life of Spirit,' I reminded myself.

The Life of Spirit has certain norms which I may disclose to you.

(i) Simplicity.

(ii) Simran (Naam Jap).

(iii) Humility.

(iv) Compassion for the poor.

(v) Gratitude to Lord under all circumstances.

These are the 'five jewels' of spiritual life.

May every one of you be blessed with these five jewels.

May you blossom with the fragrance of the Name Divine and make your life meaningful.

Every Suffering Is A Gift

I have spent a part of my life with the village folks, sharing their life style and imbibing their values. I bond with them easily. The village folks are humble, simple and natural. They are way above the urban people. They are blessed with deep devotion for the Divine. Their faith is intense and beyond any rationale. Here is an incident, I would like to narrate. I was on my daily walk, when I came upon a group of villagers engaged in a dialogue. They were debating on the question: what is the true *Ashiqi (True Love)*? The true *ashiqi* is the Love Divine. Who is the *Ashiq* (Lover)? The true lover is the one who loves the Lord. His love is focused on the Divine. It is universal love. The true lover is the one, who in spite of circumstantial sufferings, does not avert his attention from God.

I joined in this group discussion. One of the group members appeared to be a man of God. He spoke little. His eyes sparkled with radiance, and as I looked in his eyes, I felt drawn towards him like a magnet to the iron pillar. He said, "The one who loves the Lord is his true friend. He remains calm under all circumstances. He faces life's obstacles with a smile on his lips. He remains rooted in Love, even when surrounded by physical and mental adversities. He knows not what it is to be frustrated – For he accepts the will of the Lord with grace and joy. To him every suffering is a gift from his Beloved friend."

I was deeply touched by his words. I bowed down to this humble man of God. His words were priceless pearls of wisdom. He was not only humble, he was also full of love. He lived hidden in the knowledge of the spiritual life.

God Is Our Mother

One day I was in a village. I went to take bath at the local pond. On my way back, I felt a deep yearning for the Lord. 'Shyam, how do I meet you?' My heart cried out. A small voice whispered : If you want to meet the Lord, then meet the ones who have immersed themselves in the love of Lord.' On the way back I met a *Fakir*, tuning *Ek Tara*. His eyes were bright and illuminated. I fell at his feet. The '*Fakir*' asked : Child, what do you want?

I was unable to answer. I faltered with the words. '*Sai*' was all I can say. The more I gazed into his luminous eyes, the less I wanted to speak. The *Fakir* requested : 'Child ask. What do you want?'

Encouraged, I said : 'I have a longing for the Lord. Show me the path.'

The Fakir replied. 'If you want to meet the Lord, go the way of the moth. Learn to dip your soul in the spiritual colours.'

'How to do that?' I humbly asked the *Fakir*.

'The moth has an intense yearning for the light. Its yearning does not end till it burns itself in the flame. The real longing is that in which you lose yourself in the love of the Lord, you become nothing. You are ego-less.'

I share with him the agony of my heart. 'I have this longing within me. But when I introspect and look within, I find I am full of flaws. The same heart yearns and the same heart harbours evil. I scold myself – how will God accept me? How can I be accepted at the door of Heaven?'

The *Fakir* gazes into my eyes. He gives me a divine look and says, 'you are a child of God. Why do you go to the temple? In the temple, you sing the holy words. What do our scriptures say – there is one sentence in *Gurbani*; *Tum mata pita, hum balak tere.* (Thou art our Father & our Mother). That is true. You are a child. God is your father and your mother.'

He then draws a parallel between God and mother. He added :

'A child yearns to be with his mother. He is full of dirt and filth. But the moment he sees his mother, he wants to run and embrace her. The mother first wants to cleanse the child and then hug it to her heart. But the child is impatient. He is in a hurry to clasp his mother.

God is like our mother. He wants to clean and bathe his children before hugging them to his bosom. But we children are not willing to wait. We yearn to run and play in the mother's lap. We want our mother. We cry, we wail for the mother unaware of the filth we carry. The mother too cannot bear the child's cries. She hugs the child, and embraces him. If our longing is true, then even though we are filled with evil; even though we have committed sins, God will hear our plaintive cries and embrace us. He will say : Come my child. Come and play in my lap, for I love you and He will clasp you to His heart.'

'Fasting' Thoughts

One of the 'yagna' is 'fasting'. Fasting has many virtues. It helps self-control. True fasting means control over senses.

I started 'fasting' when I used to live in a small village. I lived by myself. I lived within. I 'fasted' once a week. The first time I kept 'fast', I found it difficult to restrain myself. I skipped morning breakfast. The lunch hour went by. In the night I was tempted to have a piece of *'Tosha'* (sweet) which I had seen in a box in the cupboard. I opened the cupboard and took out one piece of sweet. I beguiled myself with the words 'I have fasted the whole day. I can now have this piece of sweet'. Then I pulled up myself, garnered my will power and reminded myself that I had promised myself to abstain from food for 24 hours. I could not cheat myself! That day, though I 'fasted', and physically I did not eat food, my mind kept wavering and yearning for food. That's not called 'fasting'.

'Move On' Is The Song

Larkana in summer is like a furnace. I happened to be there one summer. In the evening we used to go to canal for a dip in the cool waters. Some of us carried baskets of sweet mangoes – small and sweet, for which Larkana is famous. We found relief from the blistering heat in the cool shade of the mango grove. On one such hot day, I took a cool dip in the canal, and rushed home immediately. I was feeling very hungry. I almost ran unable to bear the pangs of hunger. On reaching home, I found a crowd gathered near my house. Most of them were Muslims. Amidst the crowd sat a singer whose soulful singing wrenched my heart. I stood a little distance away, mesmerized by the magic of his music. Someone in the crowd recognized me and welcomed me warmly. He brought a chair and made me feel comfortable. 'Kindly sit down', he requested, adding 'we will sit on the floor. We will continue to sing for some more time.' Wonderful was their affection. As I sat down the singer's eyes hold me. The singers played on *tera cota* pitchers, used for the beat of the music. I heard one song very clearly. I still remember one line of that song. On that hot summer evening, the singer raised his voice to a crescendo crying:

'The devotee smitten by the love for the Lord
    Surrenders his life to him
And moves on; he moves on.'

The sweet memory of that song, still rings in my ears. Beautiful words. Surrender and sacrifice and move on, and on.

My Beloved Shines In My Eyes

One day I went to visit another village. I saw a group of children playing by the roadside. I was drawn to them. I loved children. I saw God's light shining in their eyes. I hear Shyam Sunder's laughter in their voices. Their innocence fascinated me. So when I saw these children playing, I went closer to them. To my anguish I found them hitting a beggar with stones. Imagine throwing stones on a *Fakir* who appeared to be a man of God. The children's play was no fun. It had hurt the *fakir* in the head and blood oozed out of that wound. I scolded the children. "stop, stop!" I said, "why are you hitting an innocent harmless beggar? What a crime! It is sinful to harm another person. Stop this violence."

One of the children had the cheek to say: "Do not interfere with us. You do not know this man. He thinks he is God! He says, I sing the holy name of God. I am with the God all the time. God is there in every breath of mine. I am God! We should murder a beggar like this who thinks he is God!"

The true meaning of the beggar's song became apparent. These children were ignorant. It was futile to argue with them. I gave them a stern look and then they stopped throwing stones at the beggar saint. The bunch of children moved closer to me. I made them sit by my side and gave each one a sweet. (I always carry sweets for children). I told them to go home. I admonished them: "never again throw stones on any beggar."

I took a few steps and went closer to the beggar; his head was bleeding profusely. I cleaned the wound and bandaged it. I asked him, "Man of God! Tell me if you need any thing."

What did this *darvesh* ask? Not money, nor possessions; he said, "I am very thirsty, give me some water to drink. There is a river nearby. You have to walk a few steps and fetch water." He handed me an earthen cup and said, "fill this with water. I am very thirsty." Surely, he must be really very thirsty for it was a hot noon. I brought the water from the nearby river. He drank the water and felt better. He spoke; what he spoke surprised me; for his were the words of wisdom. "These children have done me a favour. They threw stones to make me suffer. I am happy that they were throwing stones at me."

I asked, "Why?"

He replied, "These stones are also the gift from my Beloved, God be praised."

At this, I disclosed to him of the criminal intention of the children. "Do you know what these children were aiming at?" I asked.

"Yes, I do know that," he replied. "Even in that intention, I see the guiding hand of my Lord. Do not be angry with the children. What ever happens, happens with the will of God."

He quoted a verse :

Everything that is, is the will of God.
Everything that happens is the will of God.

I was astonished. "O God's Man! You say, that you heard the voice of Beloved in the harsh words of the children? What was that voice? What was that song that you heard from your Beloved?"

He replied, "I heard the song which I like and which I sing again and again."

"Pray sing that song for me," I pleaded with him.

The *Fakir* in his sweet melodious voice sang :

My Beloved shines in my eyes
My Beloved is the light of my heart
Why do you my Beloved, then hide from me?
Everywhere I feel Your presence, though invisible to me.
Why do you hide from me, O' my Beloved?

The *Fakir* wept as he sang. I bowed down to this beggar saint. I returned home filled with the throbbing music of his song. I kept humming the words, **my Beloved shines in my eyes and my Beloved smiles on my lips**.

On The Banks Of The Mystical Sindhu River

It was the mystic twilight hour. Earthen lamps were lit in homes, as the dusk gathers into night. At the sacred hour I sat on the banks of the river Sindhu. I watched it flow by.

I was in a small town in my own Sind province, through which this gorgeous river Sindhu flowed. I sat on its banks and reflected.

The people here were very simple. Their living was humble. But Oh Lord! Their devotion and faith was astounding. *Fakirs* and *darveshes* lived here. At this late hour, in the evening as the sun went down, rosary beads moved and prayers flowed out in the air and created an ocean of serendipity.

It was here that I witnessed a magical scene. Women of all ages had assembled on the river bank. Full of devotion, they lighted the lamps and offered worship to the flowing waters of the river. In that prayerful mood, I watched them do *aarti* (evening *Aradhana*). And I was touched and I was moved by their devotion. This group of women sitting on the river bank weaved a magic spell for me. I mused: "These sisters are much above me. May be they have not acquired English education, may be they have not learnt economics, but they are rich in the spiritual knowledge of devotion and faith."

Each sister carried a tiny lamp, her eyes glowing in the radiance of that beam of light. A waft of breeze blew and snuffed some of the tiny flames. And yet the sisters continued with their prayerful worship. They recited the *aarti* of Guru Nanak in a sweet melodious voice. These sisters came from humble homes. They were simple village women. But their faith was immense. Their song rejuvenated my heart, as I stood on the banks of that magnificent river, at twilight hour with little lamps floating on the river, the sound of the sacred chant of Guru Nanak reverberated the air. All of it was an intensely mystical experience. The words of that song were as beautiful as its meaning.

> I am a seeker at your door!
> My soul thirsts for your grace.
> Can I ask for more?

Three Priceless Pearls

Once, I went to a village and there met many simple folks. They asked me to give them a teaching. I told them, "I am still a student. I am still learning. How can I teach you anything? Yes, I can pass on to you the teachings of my revered Master and my Gurudev."

My Master called me one day. He gave me three teachings which were like priceless pearls.

1) Be like salt.

2) Be like a house.

3) Be like light.

The villagers were perplexed. They asked, "Sir, kindly explain to us what this means?"

To them I explained :

1) Be like salt.

My dear ones. It is so hot here. Without salt, our food would be insipid. Salt adds taste to food. So you should also be like salt; add something to your self and your surroundings.

2) Be like a house.

House protects us in the night from burglars. It keeps us safe 'inside', from rain and sunshine. We should be like a house and protect the weak and the downtrodden.

3) Be like light.

Light or illumination is the symbol of knowledge. Light of knowledge dispels darkness of ignorance, and shows the path. We must hold the lamp for others.

The villagers in their utter simplicity, asked, "What is our duty?"

I replied, "To protect the weak; to show the light to those floundering in darkness. For all this you have to improve yourself, make your life pure and accept the will of God under all circumstances."

Dialogue With A *Fakir* - The Flame Of Love

At the break of dawn, I entered my small room, and sat in silence. I reflected on the purpose of life. The more I pondered over it, the deeper I was dragged into a pool of undefined sorrow. At this juncture, I remember my dialogue with the *Fakir*.

"O *Fakir Sai*," I had asked him, "What does God need? What gift shall I give him?"

The *Fakir* had replied, "O dear one, I had put the same question to my *Mursheed*, my Master. My Master who is ever so merciful, ever so benevolent, who eternally illuminates the Sun, the Moon and the Stars. The One who ever smiles on earth, had replied : O seeker I need but one Gift."

"O Master, tell me which Gift?" I had asked eagerly.

"My Master *Rehman* Sai said, give God the gift of a sorrowful heart," replied the *fakir*.

I sat in silence in my room. I plunged into sorrow which is difficult to describe. This sorrow tears me apart; I am unable to bear it, I weep, I cry. Crying helps; it cleanses the heart and purifies it. Suddenly my heart begins to throb. It pounds so hard that I fear a cardiac arrest. I am dazed and then out of the blue, I see a flash of light blaze by. The light is bright like an electric light but its illumination dazzles me. I gaze out of the window and see the stars shining in the sky. Outside it is a pitch dark night and I realise that I have been sitting inside the closed room since the early hours of the dawn.

I look outside; I gaze at the star spangled sky. One particular star is radiantly bright. What illumination, what light have you brought for me, I ask of it.

In the stillness of the night I weep again. I hear a whispering voice. Do not cry my dear. And don't puzzle yourself. Just look up at that glowing star. The same radiant light shines within you. Bring the same light into your life, in your daily chores and in your daily living. I realised then, that light was no ordinary light. It was an illuminating light which blazoned through the room and faded into oblivion touching my soul, and stirring my heart for ever. The name of that illuminating light is flame of love. Take this flame far and wide and sing the name of God. That is the purpose of life.

A *Fakir's* Song

During my stay in Sind, I had visited a small village by the name of Sultan Kot. The people of this village were warm and affectionate. They welcomed me with sincerity and love. Their genuine love fascinated me. I stayed with the Hakim of the village.

Early next morning, there was a knock on my door. I opened it. To my surprise, a fakir stood on the steps of the house. From my early childhood I had great attraction for the *fakirs*, sages and seers: my soul longed for them, my heart yearned for their company. The *fakir* was holding an '*Ektara*'. I took him inside the room and made him sit on the chair. The *fakir* did not disclose his identity but humbly said, 'Would you like to hear a song? I sing the songs of Raodas.'

He rendered a hymn like song in his mellifluous voice. His eyes moved and rested on a flower lying on the table, Looking at it, he whispered, "May I please have it? You are anyway going to throw it." He picked up the flower, kissed it several times and spoke to it. 'O my beloved. O the king of my heart.' His eyes were brimmed with tears. He kissed the flower again and again. What identification with God, what reverence for His creation! He had expressed his love for God's creation by pouring his love to a withering flower. I was touched by this man's insight. Reflecting on this, I went back to my room. Moved, I too expressed my emotions in a poem.

> Day in, and day out, I wandered,
> I saw You on the mountain peak,
> I climbed, for my heart belongs to those who understand God!
>
> The darkness of night fades
> But the longing in my heart
> Grows intense even at the dawn,
>
> For my heart yearns for those,
> Who hail from the other shore.
> Who is He, who calls me,
> Who is He, who showers His mercy on me,
> Ah, My heart chases those, who have seen the door –

O Beloved, I would leave all,
And suffer no end, only to be with you
For I seek those, who are on the path.
Come Beloved mine, and be a king of my heart
Sing the song of spirit, I may never be apart
from you my Beloved!

For my heart craves for those who have seen the Eternal light
Oh, Nuri, I have waited long, wounded and bruised,
My Beloved, hug me to your heart, ferry me into that realm of Light.

A True Sufi

On a hot summer day I heard the sweet sound of *Tambura* being played outside my room. A *fakir* gingerly entered my room. He made himself comfortable. *Fakirs* and Mendicants are natural people without the sophistication of urban etiquette. They are above worldly niceties. Intoxicated by love divine they wandered from place to place. They were intuitively drawn to special people and places. They went there to bless them. This *fakir* too had been drawn to me. He delighted me with his heart wrenching music. A true *sufi*, he sang the *Kalams* of Sachal and Bedil. This mystic beloved of God came for a short while, but left behind an everlasting impact on this humble soul.

During those days, I had a mystical love for Krishna. Yet so touched was I by this Muslim *Fakir*, that I could hear Krishna's flute playing in his *sufi Kalams*. As he was leaving, I requested him for his address. He obliged. Few days passed by. I went to this *Fakir's* house: a humble hut on the banks of a river. I bowed down to him and sought his blessings. What he said to me has faded from my memory. But I have poeticised his teaching as:

> I have no devotee,
> I am not a Guru
> Day and night,
> *I meditate on my Sat-Guru.*
> *He alone deserves my love,*
> He alone commands my heart,
> To seek his grace and a merciful glance
> Is my only yearning, my only need.

The Fakir explained : Since I am not a Guru, I do not have devotees. His words surprised me. He uttered *Satguru* with such reverence! A Muslim talking of *Satguru*? A Muslim talking of spiritual treasures which only a *Satguru* could bestow on his disciples? "The spiritual treasure is a rare diamond. It is beyond compare." Overwhelmed, I chatted with the *Fakir*, "You may not be a Satguru but aren't you a *Fakir*?" I asked him. At this tears welled up in his eyes. He admitted that he was a *Fakir*. It was my good fortune to have met such a divine soul in that small village, in Sind.

The Mystic Fakir

The night had just ended. It was still dark. The dawn was about to break. I heard a cry, a distinct cry of pain and agony. It wrenched my heart. I went out to find the source of that cry which had pierced my heart. A poor man lying on the floor of his hut was calling out: Is there a man of God?

I asked him, "O beloved, what is it you want?"

He replied, " I have lost my eye sight. I am blind. I am calling out to a holy man who would perform the miracle of restoring my vision, so that I can see once again. I desire to get back my eye sight. I wish to see again." This call of mercy puts me in a dilemma. I asked him, "Do you have any other desire of the same intensity?"

"Yes," he replied, "if I cannot get back the sight, I would like to have the vision of the heart. I would like to open and see the lotus of my heart."

"What do you mean by the lotus of your heart?" I asked him.

He explained: "I desire that I should be filled with so much compassion that I can forgive people. I should give them the love of my heart unconditionally."

This man longed for what is known in the spiritual parlance as 'the understanding heart'.

Believe me, this was the need of the hour. In today's turbulent world, where tempers fly high, and hatred and envy have gripped our life, what we need is 'the understanding'. I am reminded of that great historical figure, King Solomon. In those ancient times, India had trade relations and political connections with King Solomon's kingdom. What did King Solomon pray for? His only prayer was 'O! Lord! Give me the love of an understanding heart!'

One of the reasons why there is so much conflict in the world is lack of understanding hearts. The rulers of the states do not understand the poor people's problems;

they do not have understanding hearts. Ironically, I received this insight from a visually impaired man in this small village. An insight which forms the crux of my teachings : Give sympathy : Give the love of an understanding heart. Give compassion and love to all.

God Lives In Every Human Being

During my village sojourns, I was once a guest in a teacher's house. The school was small and had very few students. But the children had bright faces with shining eyes. I felt I should spend some more time in their company.

One day I found a total chaos in the village. The air was thick with tension. I wondered what was wrong with this small peaceful village? I checked out with the students and learnt that there was a visitor, whom the students loved greatly. He was highly respected by the community. The villagers were very happy to have him, but unfortunately, this time his visit had misfired. This visitor had mingled with the untouchables. He had even prayed with them, chanted the Holy name with them. He accepted the *Prasad* and ate it. The villagers were disgusted. The village panchayat met and warned the villagers of dire consequences, if they gave the visitor even a glass of water. They forbade the villagers from visiting him. Their argument was: He belongs to the untouchables, and we have nothing to do with such a man.

'Alaa Alaa ! My Lord !' The villagers pleaded with them,' "this man is so dear to us. We think he is God's good man. But our village Panchs have brought restrictions on us ! O God ! now what to do?" They felt despondent. "How can we not meet him?" They said, with tearful eyes. When I learnt of the incident I felt very sad. That night I visited the untouchables. Their '*kirtan*' was ecstatic. I was deeply moved. They met me with great affection. They were happy because I had visited their humble commune, without any formal invitation.

"Oh dear man of God, you have brought tons of blessings with you. What service may we offer to you?" they asked. I was touched by their humility. I felt like weeping. I requested them to give me a broom. They were surprised. Taking the broom I went into their settlement. It was littered with filth. I went to each and every hut and cleaned it. The Harijans felt very happy. They said, "Dear one you are our true brother. You have taught us a great lesson. May we be worthy of those tears in your eyes."

After sweeping the huts clean I gave them a simple message. **Service of the Harijans is the worship of God.** The words had magical effect on them. And as they gathered in the *satsang*, they hummed together :

Harijano ki seva hai
Prabhu ki pooja

It was a touching scene. As they sang, they wept tears of devotion. The villagers realised the truth of those words. My tears and their tears mingled to bear witness to that truth. The truth being, that the same God exists in every human being.

Darvesh Of Rohiri

Once I had the opportunity to visit the holy town of Rohiri. There by good fortune I ran into a *Darvesh*. He was very fair and well built like a *Pathan*. But unlike *pathan*s his face glowed with an unusual radiance. I had a dialogue with him. Some of his words penetrated my heart. A great soul, he gifted me the following teachings. He said : 'Have faith in God.'

To this I argued : 'Man errs. What indicates that he has erred? How are we to know that we have turned away from the right path?'

His reply was simple : 'If a man forsakes the path of spirituality, the hollowness of his life troubles him. His conscience pricks him. Such pricks of consciousness are signs of being distracted away from the path of God.'

The second teaching pertains to our daily life. He said, 'forgive the sins and omissions of those who serve you.'

How many times? I asked.

The *Darvesh* looks at me and says, 'Not once, not twice, but 70 times you must forgive. If your servant has erred, you forgive him every day.'

The third teaching: 'Be truthful. Do not eschew the truth. Remember the All omnipresent God is listening to it. If there are three persons talking, be sure, there is the fourth one present there, and he is Allah! So be careful of what you think and what you speak. Don't be a victim of illusions. Hold to truth as the sinking boat holds to the buoyant.'

The fourth teaching: 'Remember the omnipotent, the omnipresent Lord! This entire Universe is an expression of God's love. It is a paean to His grace. Every creature sings his name. At the break of dawn, birds warble, spreading their wings they take to the skies, every creature sings the praises of the Lord. So O human being, do not be ignorant. Acknowledge your existence by praising God.'

The fifth teaching: 'Be aware of the end. Know well the time is running out on all of us. Do not delay. For when the journey ends God should not say 'It is too late. I was ill you did not serve me. I was hungry, you did not feed me.'

I humbly asked the *Darvesh*, "Sir how can God fall ill? God is free of all negativity."

The *Darvesh* replies, "My dear one, perhaps you do not know that he resides in all, he lives in all. If anyone falls ill and you do not serve him, it is like not serving God."

The sixth teaching: 'One more thing is necessary if you are on the spiritual path. That is charity. Give alms in charity without the thought of receiving praise or acknowledgement. Give all in charity. Do so secretly. Quietly go and serve the poor with love in your heart.

The seventh teaching: 'Give them your love. Love has a magic quality. It can turn copper into gold. Love heals. Even the kings and emperors who have compassion in their heart serve the poor with immense love. Without love everything is dust. Love is the only truth. Love is the only reality. Everything else is meaningless. Let love illuminate your heart.

Love is God.

I gazed into the burning eyes of this mystic *Darvesh* and bid him a fond farewell. "*Khuda Hafis*". Long live O holy man of God, I prayed loudly.

Four Words

Many years ago I visited a co-educational school. I was requested to address the students. A prominent man who was also the head of the school organisation whispered in my ears, "Do speak. But speak only four words."

Which four words did I speak?

The four words are :

    Speak the truth
    Play games
    Serve the poor
    Remember to recite the holy name of God.

My Little Walk

Many years ago, I was walking along the road. I found a child crying. I went up to it and asked, "My dear child, what makes you cry?" The child replied, "I am searching for my mother." The child had gone out to run an errand for his mother. On his way back he had lost the way. The child was calling out to his mother. The child did not remember the address nor the location of his house. This only made our task difficult. After a massive search, we located the child's house. Reaching the child home made me feel happy. Seeing the joy of the mother and the child and their reunion, I felt elevated. Emotionally moved I penned down a few words after I returned home.

My little walk
My little task
O Lord this I offer as
Worship unto thee!

Let other seekers go to temples and ring the bells. Let others go to shrines and light the lamps. For me serving a poor child and reaching him safely home is a true prayer, it is my worship unto Thee O Lord!

God Of Small Things

I am referring to a period when Gandhism was very popular. In every village, in every house, people used to run '*charkha*' and spin the cotton thread. The spinning wheel was Gandhiji's symbol of independence (self reliance). I happened to visit a village which thrived on this cottage industry. There I met a widow. She shared her sorrow. The words she told me impressed me so much that I put them into a poem :

I turn the spinning wheel
I spin the yarn,
Singing in devotion your songs,
My humble offering to you
My Beloved!

I considered this widow a fortunate one for she had found her devotion, her prayers, and her worship in the little things of life. The simple activity of spinning the cotton yarn was her offering to God.

Work is worship. God feels happy even at the little acts of life done with devotion of the heart.

Many years ago I was in Bengal. People had gathered together to celebrate the colourful festival of Holi. They sang and danced with devotion. Cymbals clashed. Dancing with joy people swirled as they gathered around a beautifully decorated crib. I went closer to it.

What did I see? Inside the crib was the sacred idol of Krishna. Devotees were swaying in ecstasy, singing and dancing they rocked the crib. Their joyful singing went to my heart. Even though the song was in Bengali, I have managed to translate it in Sindhi :

My Shyam Sunder, let my lullaby,
And the beautiful silken strings with which I embellish you
Be my offering, my worship O Shyam Sunder.

Small joys for God of small things. Spinning the wheel or helping the child to reach home or rocking the cradle of the Lord, may seem inconsequential acts but if done with devotion they are the true worship of God. God is pleased by small acts of kindness more than gigantic rituals, such as *yagna*. The true *yagna* is one that which purifies. Small acts of devotion which purify us and fill us with joy, are true *yagna*.

Humbly I present these views to you, for I firmly believe that our happiness lies in doing small acts of kindness. Therefore I urge you devotees of the Lord, to do small acts of devotion; give up the thoughts of doing large projects which will only heighten your ego.

A rich man once invited me to a *yagna* being performed at a particular place. He insisted that I attend it. He proudly said that he had spent more than a thousand rupees on it. A thousand rupees for a *yagna*? O God, I prayed. Let me be an instrument of thy actions. Let me be your servant and be at the service of the poor and the lowly. That is true *yagna*. The *yagna* of service.

Let me narrate an incident which has touched my heart deeply. It is about a young girl of 19 years who had an old ailing mother. This young girl finds a job in a rich man's house. Her job is to do chores like sweeping the floor and washing the utensils. She did this to earn enough to take care of her mother. She had an intense desire to visit a temple. But she had no time. She reasons out thus, "My temple is the house where I work, my shrine is the place I clean and look after." She calls out to the Lord: O' God all this work I do is my worship to you; and the place I worship is your temple.

I felt sympathy for this girl. So moved was I by her attitude that I poetisized her words,

O! God of small things
Every thing I do, is my devotion
Every where I work is my Shrine,
In mercy keep me, in mercy bind!

Look at the devotion of the simple girl. She finds God in small acts of cleaning utensils, in washing the floors; she sees the Lord in the beautiful rays of dawn; in the sunset hours of the twilight. She feels enriched taking care of an old woman. She feels God in polishing the shoes; in the labour of sweeping the place. I think of this young girl as a *Brahmagyani*, for whatever she does, she feels the presence of God. She pleads to the Lord to keep her as she is, in the same circumstances and under the same conditions.

> May I find your Love
> In the simple act of cooking.
> May I get a glance of you
> As I clean the vessels
> May I rejoice in these simple
> Acts of devotion.
> Oh! Nuri, I surrender
> My work to you.
> For this is my true Karma!

This is the last stage of spiritual progress: a stage where one feels that work is worship of God.

The question arises whether we can reach this stage; whether we can achieve this goal? Personally I feel, it is not necessary to ring the bells in temple or light the joss sticks. What is required, is to make our daily work into acts of worship.

Different Prayers, Different Worship

A saint was walking on the road. The road was lonely and the saint was alone. Out of the blue, shrill cries rent the air – move away, and move away, for a leper is coming this way. In those days a leper was considered an untouchable and an outcast. People did not want even to cross his shadow. But this saint hears the cries and instead of moving away, goes closer to the leper and bows down to him. He pulls out a few rupees from his pocket and hands them to the leper, "please accept this" he says humbly.

He then cleanses the wounds of the leper, gives him water to drink and what does he say to him? 'You too are an image of God'. What comforting words! This saint believed that, service of the poor is worship of God!

•••••

Once many years ago, I had a dialogue with a millionaire. He had invited me home. He said, "You preach great many things. But let me tell you, there are some of your teachings which I dislike."

I asked him the reason for not liking my teachings. He replied, " You keep asking people to pray. Why should I pray? I have enough wealth, enough to feed the future five generations. I have no need to pray. I am well settled in my life and enjoy the respect of people."

This man who lived in a large luxurious house with a manicured garden asks, 'why should I pray? I have no faith in God. Besides, I have everything that I desire, - wealth, status and fame!' I was a guest in this man's house for a short while. He looked after me very well. He was very generous in his hospitality. Nevertheless he kept saying that he had no faith in God and had no need to pray.

What could I say to him? I thought it against my moral etiquette to discuss God with him. He was my honourable, impeccable host. I smiled away at his ignorance.

•••••

I stayed in Sakhar for a brief period. Sakhar gets very hot in summer, and the place really sizzles with heat. On one such hot, sweltering afternoon, a man with *tamboora* entered my room. He was strumming the strings. I looked up at him and asked, "Who are you my dear friend."

He replied, "I am a *Fakir*. I am a devotee of a *Sufi Pir*, I am a Muslim. But I have great affection for Hindus."

I asked him the reason for his love for Hindus.

He replied: "There is only one reason. He, the Almighty dwells in both, Hindus and Muslims."

This man, dressed in a single robe, wrapped in a coarse *chaddar* impressed me. Such a simple man, with such a sweet melodious voice! His *chaddar* holds my attention. The *Fakir* read the question in my mind and answered, "*Sai* in summer I wear this coarse cloth as a *chaddar*, in winter I use it as a blanket. The *chaddar* or blanket serves as a mat in day and a cover in the night. My food is '*satvic*'. I eat wild berries and curds. I live by the river bank in a straw hut; but believe me it is as good as a palace for me."

He said he gets sound sleep in his straw hut, perhaps even kings and queens may not be getting such good sleep in their luxurious palaces.

I glanced at the *tamboora* and felt the need to hear music. I requested him to sing me a song. "I would like to hear a *Sufi Kaafi* or a *Doha*."

I believe that God resides in the tender loving songs of the villagers. The villagers are natural and more spontaneous in their emotions than we city bred people are.

The *Fakir's* song touched my soul. His mellifluous voice enchanted me. The *Fakir* was humble, exuding warmth of love divine. I was moved by the spirituality of the words he sang. I wept tears, for the depth of his words made me feel inadequate inside of me.

O Miya Omar,
Do not snatch away
My hand woven blanket
Wild berries and curds are
My food,
I know not the taste of *Pulav* (rice preparation),
O Miya Omar,
Do not snatch away
My humble diet.
I will not seek another lover,
My only lover is my husband
O Miya Omar
Do not tear me apart from him
Lest I may die of separation.

The closer I went to this *Fakir*, the greater was my loving appreciation for him. His teachings built on two pillars of simplicity and chanting God's name impressed me.

•••••

One day this *Fakir* takes me to his home. We go over the earth toll on the banks of Sindhu. His humble hut is above the placid waters of the river. It has a serenity which prompts me to ask, "Sir, who is your spiritual Master?"

He humbly replies, "The spiritual leader is only one. *Allah* is the Alpha; but we are unable to see his radiance."

He points his index finger to a gentle woman sitting in a corner. Her face has the glow of a mystical light. Her face beams out a rare serenity. She greets me with a few words and ushers me inside the thatched hut. She brings us water to drink. It is cool and sweetly soothing. I feel as if I am under the cooling gush of a waterfall. Our peace is disturbed by the interruption of an unknown man. He rushes in and bursts into tears. The saintly woman dearly enquires of him:

"Why do you cry so much? What has happened?"

The man weeps, "I am ruined. I am finished."

I do not wish to go into the details of their conversation. The gist of it all is, that this man had fallen in love with a woman. He sins. He finds it difficult to come out of this torrid affair. The fire of passion consumes him and devastates him. He keeps falling into the pit of passion. He sins. The burden of it is too heavy. He is unable to bear the guilt load. His remorse brings him to this saintly woman. "Release me from this pit of fire, or else I will become ashes," he implores her.

Hearing this, the saintly woman smiles. She places her hand on his head and says, "O my dear brother, there is fire in every passion. Remember God is compassionate and ever forgiving. Remember even this fire of passion is His doing and to extinguish it, will also be His doing."

The man is perplexed by this answer. "How can God shower the waters of his mercy on the burning fire of this sinner?"

This saintly woman says, "One tear of repentance can extinguish this fire. A tear of repentance can wash away all your sins. It can revive you to be your own self. Repentance is a great purifier."

This man finds solace in these words. Just as a tired thirsty traveler quenches his thirst by cool waters of the stream, similarly this man is redeemed of his burden of sin. The saintly woman, had blessed him with the Waters of the Spirit.

Pearl Of Peace

The incident I am going to narrate occurred when I was in Sakhar. I was staying with a rich family. The head of the family was a learned lawyer. He earned thousands of rupees every month. Every morning after taking his bath, he would enter worship room which enshrined Guru Granth Sahib. He read from it religiously before beginning his day's work. He took his daily guidance from a random page *vachan* opened from the Guru Granth Sahib.

I found a similar practice of this early morning reading from *Gurbani* in another lawyer's house, in another city. In spite of his hectic schedule, this lawyer too began the day with the recitation of *Gurbani*.

Sri Sukhmani Sahib is an important chapter in the Guru Granth Sahib. Sri Sukhmani Sahib is a rich treasure of wisdom, written in a lyrical way. It provides many insights into the outer/inner realms of life. It is a text of devotion. I wish every one of you to posses a copy of it. Carry it in your pocket and whenever time permits, open it at random and read the contents. Reflect on its meaning. It will help you in many ways.

Every now and then, I read Sri Sukhmani Sahib. I also do random chanting. Every time I open the book, I get a fresh insight into its meaning. Guru's words are like the utterances of God. Open at random and the coincidence of the text contents and the questions pestering the mind, is revealing. I marvel at the answers I receive from these sacred verses.

One of the teachings of this Scripture is to put out the fire. So many fires burn within us. There is the fire of anger, fire of passion, fire of greed, fire of ego, and fire of attachment. How to extinguish the fire?

Guru Nanak reveals: Seek the company of saints. Live in fellowship. This will not only purify your hearts but will bring calmness to your turbulent mind. Sri Sukhmani Sahib works as a soothing balm on the scorched burns of your mind and soul.

Flame Of Love

On the sacred Ram Navmi day, I picked up the Gita and opened it at random. It opened at part four. Its words penetrated my heart. It read as –

> Oh Arjuna if you seek knowledge; do so with devotion.
> Search it, and serve at His lotus feet,
> You will behold the light of the Universe.

It was the sacred Ram Navmi day and this happened long time ago. As the sun went down, the red dusty twilight set in. I sat by the side of my elder brother. I wept silent tears, for I could see the hurt in my brother's eyes. His frozen expression disturbed me. He appeared to be sleeping at that juncture. I recalled his words, "Life is to be shared. To live is to give. Serve the poor and be their friend."

The *Rishis* and the *Vedas* invoke the blessings, "May you not be separated from the loved ones". I tried to control my emotions.

Many years ago, I had asked my brother a pertinent question, "Which is the most important need of the hour?"

He had replied, "India needs men of action and not orators. India needs men who would work in silence; who would be humble and simple; who would feel concerned about the poor people."

We must serve the poor. I have great love for the simple village people. I am in search of those simple students. A little voice within me whispers, where are such students? Where are those simple children? Go and find them.

My brother had a noble heart. In that heart burnt a flame; *The flame of Love.*

Every day his thoughts went out to the simple poor people of rural India. This became his daily prayer. That day my beloved brother passed away. He left his mortal body for the eternal shore. The sun was going down and the darkness deepened as I watched my beloved brother leave for journey onward. His sojourn on this earth plane was over. He had moved on to heavenly home.

That night when I entered my room, I went into silence. My body was tired and weary. In that silence my mind carried on a dialogue with my brother. Truly, your life is a primer for me, for I have learnt many a lesson from you. I remember those beautiful words which you spoke but which were really meant for me. "The path of Gita is threefold.

The first is to keep your hand open. Give, give and keep giving.

The second is, always speak the truth and harm no one.

The third is to live a life of compassion and service.

These three stages in the path of Gita are an important landmark in evolutionary development of mankind.

My brother had said, "Go and teach this to your students and just as a tree gives many seeds and many seeds give many trees, so shall your word spread and transform many lives."

On that day, the last day of his earthly journey, I found an unusual radiance on his face; a brightness difficult to describe. Perhaps it was the glow of his spirituality. Perhaps it was the eternal flame which had shone the splendour of light in his life. May our young generation — students in schools and colleges, in universities and institutions — be in quest of knowledge and more knowledge. May their lives be illuminated by my brother's vision. I thank God for bestowing His blessings and blessing me with such a brother. After I bid a tearful adieu to my brother, I wrote a poem which is indeed a paean of tribute to his great soul.

Ways Of A Wanderer

I am in the city of Hyderabad (Sind), all alone, and seriously ill. I am down with pneumonia and feeling low. However I do not feel the need for calling a doctor or of informing anyone. I like to be by myself; for my companion, my guardian, my protector and my friend is always there by my side.

Three days later, the well-known doctor Dr. Tharumal comes to know of my illness. Immediately he visits me and expresses his deep concern. I assure him that I am all right and nothing is seriously wrong with me. He is not convinced. After thorough checkup, he gives me a worried look. "The pneumonia has struck your lungs, it is no small thing. You better be careful... Do not play with your life; your life is very precious," he says.

His genuine concern touches my heart. He suggests that I shift to his house. "Living here alone will worsen your condition; you better shift to my house." And without a moment's hesitation he goes out, hires a Tonga and takes me home. He keeps me in a separate section of his bungalow and makes me feel comfortable.

My Gurudev had said, "When you are ill, then the doctor is your God. "Listen to him and take his advice."

To me Dr. Tharumal was verily an image of God. His affection and concern went far beyond the doctor's duties.

"Please stay here till you fully regain your strength. It may take months ..." he says tenderly.

Dr. Tharumal looked after me, as a mother would look after her child. True indeed, during those three months of my illness he was my God.

•••••

Whenever I was in the city of Hyderabad I used to visit a particular temple every month. Sometimes, I even gave discourses on the temple premises. One day with the kind permission of the presiding priest, I invited a few harijans to join me in the *'Naam'* kirtan.

Since they were special invitees we prepared for them special *'Prasad'*. The *'harijans'* were happy to participate in the *kirtan* program. They also enjoyed the *'Prasad'* especially made for them.

Hell broke loose after they had left. The presiding priest was furious. The news of *harijans* chanting the sacred name of the Lord in the temple precincts, spread like wild fire. Sharp reaction from the public unnerved the presiding priest. He confronted me with many questions and called me names.

I was frank with him and told him that whatever had happened had happened with his consent. "We have done service to humanity, it cannot be branded as evil." This was the whole truth.

"True I had granted you the permission, but please from the next month onwards you need not take the trouble of visiting the temple," he said this with a finality which puzzled me.

A person who does a good deed, who labours in the lord's vine-yard selflessly is unafraid of criticism! He is detached from his action and does not bother about the social reaction or of the consequences thereof.

Even then, I found it rather difficult to accept the verdict of the presiding priest. According to me, *'He hath no caste no creed. All are equal in his eyes.'*

In the Bhagavad Gita, Sri Krishna says to Arjuna, do your *dharma* without any expectation. Do not swerve from the path of Truth. The path of Truth to me is *dharma*. *Do your Karma with a feeling of Oneness.*

Years ago I founded an *ashram* in Rajpur near Mussouri which I called *Shakti Ashram*. The *Shakti Ashram* was meant to be a family— a fellowship of brothers and sisters. The day at the *ashram* began with *satsang*, which was followed by discourse. In the evening too we had *satsang*. The *ashram* had a strict rule; that is to observe absolute silence in the *satsang* hall. After the *satsang* every evening we used to sit in silence and meditate. Normally, we meditated and reflected on the message of the discourse. We would receive guidance out of the depths of silence. This silent period of reflection was often an enriching spiritual experience. We often exchanged notes and discussed and deliberated on the noble lives of saints and sages.

Silence has great spiritual value. In silence we receive the blessings of saints and sages. In silence we are able to see the illuminated path of life. In silence many unseen things are revealed. The unmanifest becomes manifest. Today the world is caught in the grip of hectic activity. In the rush for existence we forget to sing the name Divine. May we remain in the world. Yet amidst the vortex of activity, may we ever remember the Lord and his name Divine.

Every summer I spent three months at Rajpur. People from all walks of life and from all over the country would spend the summer months at the *Shakti Ashram*. One day a man came to meet me. He had brought a letter from a lady in Dehradun. He requested me to read it and give a reply immediately. I opened the letter with trembling hands. I shivered to read it. Do you know the reason? This letter was from a woman whom I wished to avoid. Years ago when I was in Calcutta, I had given a discourse at a well-attended function. As was the custom in those days, the men were seated in the hall and the women were seated in the gallery. Among the female audience was a young girl who was fascinated by my speech. Later in the day she sent me a note, telling me that she came from an aristocratic family, and that she was the daughter of a minister. After listening to my lecture she had resolved that if she had to marry, she would marry me and me alone. So possessed was she with the idea, that she sent me a photograph of herself. I was least interested. Folding hands, I prayed to the Almighty to protect me and keep me safe in His divine grace. It was this same lady who now sent me the letter through the messenger to the Ashram. In the letter she reintroduced herself, stating that she was the same person who had wished to marry me. Further she wrote: I am still unmarried, I am the principal of a school in Dehradun and I wish to meet you. I apologised to the messenger and expressed my inability to meet the lady in person. God is great; He saved me from an awkward situation.

Several years ago I faced the same situation in England. A highly talented and well-educated lady had proposed to me for marriage. She too had vowed that if she would marry, she would marry me alone. Even at that time, I had prayed to God to keep me safe. He helped me to avoid that unpleasant situation. After that incident I did not speak to that lady.

I recall another incident that took place at the Ashram. Amongst the inmates of the Ashram were two Americans. One day they came up to my room, and requested me to accompany them to Mussouri. I was reluctant to go with them, however they insisted. They had taken a friend's bungalow in Mussouri for a few days. They wished that I too join them on the trip. After much persuasion I agreed. The bungalow was located on a solitary hilltop. The clouds floated around making it look mystical.

I love hills and mountains. Their solitude is blissful. Hence, I enjoyed living in that beautiful bungalow, touching the floating clouds and relishing the beauty of nature.

A day after our arrival, the two American ladies came to see me in my room, and requested me to accompany them to the cinema house to view a movie. I politely refused them, but the two American ladies insisted, saying that they could not leave me alone in the bungalow. I would be lost in that far off desolate place as they would be late in coming.

I assured that I would not be lost because I love nature's solitude. I would rather prefer to be alone than to accompany them to the cinema. They began to argue highlighting the pros and cons of watching a movie.

After an hour's debate I was able to convince them that cinema was not the right thing for me because, all kinds of people gather there and many of them carry evil thoughts and have vicious intentions.

These are my humble views. Keep away from all the evil, for evil is the reason for hell. I pray may we all be away from the dark energies. May we turn to Shyam Sunder and make our life radiant with positive and pure energies.

I loved to stay in Rajpur. It is a small town; its people are either farmers, or petty shopkeepers. They are simple and good folks. Another reason, why I loved to spend summer at Rajpur is the Shakti Ashram. It became a venue for interaction with great scholars, intellectuals, and seekers. Men of great learning came from all over the country, from Calcutta, Allahabad, Madras, Agra, Lucknow and Delhi. We discussed and debated on the teachings of Sri Bhagavad Gita, Upanishads, and Vedas and other holy scriptures.

At the Ashram came to stay a woman with a small child. I was told that she was unhappy, trapped as she was in the anguish of sorrow. She was feeling low and miserable. The inmates further requested me, to visit her. I went to see her in her room. She was a young widow, clinging to her child, holding him tight in her embrace.

"Throw the child on the floor." I urged her. She looked at me, totally stunned. "What's wrong with you? How can I throw my child on the floor?" she retorted angrily. "I said, throw the child on the floor...............How much money do you need for throwing away the child?" I asked her coolly.

She was petrified. "I need as many rupees as there are stars in the sky! You cannot count the stars. They are beyond count. I need that many rupees. Come what may, I shall not throw my child on the floor!" she replied firmly.

"What's the reason?"

"You ask me the reason? The reason is obvious. I love my child beyond your comprehension. My love has no end, no limit. It is limitless."

"Well said, my sister. God is like you. His love for his children is limitless. We are all God's children and he loves us just the way you love your child. *'Tum mata pita, hum balak tere.'* You are our mother and father. We are your children. God too loves you, as you love your child. He will ferry you across the difficulties of life; he will protect you as you protect your child, provided you have faith in him and accept everything that happens in life as His grace."

She listened to me carefully.

"God loves you. Don't despair; don't be depressed." I exhort her. My words worked magic on her. She brightened up. A new positive energy flowed through her. She turned a new leaf. May each one of us build faith in God, and His doings. We should assure ourselves.

He will not cast us aside; he will not throw us away. Whatever He does is for our good. He will help us to tide over the difficulties of life and cross the hurdles; He will shower His Grace and Mercy on us. He will hold us in his embrace; may He protect us – against the turmoil of life and steer us safely to the other shore.

•••••

There was a time when I wandered from place to place, from village to village and from town to town. I roamed the countryside, trudged the fields and climbed the mountains. I did this to be closer to Him, my Beloved. I strolled on the beaches; I walked the banks on Ganges and other rivers only to be in tune with his creation.

I remember an incident. I happened to pass through a town called Nirmalnagar. Others call it Haridwar the Gateway to God. I am a pilgrim in this City of God. Even though I had many friends' acquaintances in the city I did not inform anyone of them of my visit.

On reaching Haridwar I feel hungry. During that phase of my life I used to have only one meal a day. I found a lodge and had a meal costing one *anna*. The meal consisted of one chapatti and vegetable. I was not that poor; but I had resolved to live as a Sadhu eating a frugal meal a day. This was my Sadhana.

In Haridwar I knew an *ashram* which would have given me a descent accommodation; but I preferred to be on my own, and live on one chapatti a day.

One day as I sat down to have my meal, I heard a sweet melodious voice. I was curious to know the person who had such a sweet rich voice. I asked the person sitting next to me, who is the singer? I went out to see the person. Lo and behold standing outside was a beautiful woman. So beautiful that I was stunned. I had never seen such a beauty anywhere. The woman stood there singing, her hair were uncombed, her clothes torn and tattered. Her rich soul wrenching voice shuddered me, bringing tears to my eyes. Even the people around, having meals at this lodge, were deeply touched. I do not remember the exact words of her song but whatever she was singing was spiritually very moving. The words perhaps were, Beloved oh! Beloved.

Those two words worked like magic on me. The woman's beauty, her yearning, her soulful song had mesmerized me. I wish, you my devotees, had seen and heard that voice! To me she was nothing less than a Divine Mother. Indeed she was a Divine soul, who had descended from the land of light. This woman, a rare soul, roamed the streets of Hardiwar unmindful of the stones thrown at her, very often her feet were scrapped and bruised by stones.

'Oh dear my beloved, You are the reflection of Eternal fame!'

This beautiful woman extolled the virtues of spiritual beauty. Beauty is not only external but also internal. A truly beautiful human being is one who is beautiful from within and from without.

A well-known philosopher has said - O' God bless me with inner beauty. A humble song, when translated reads as:

O' my dear one, O' my beloved,
O' the divine reflection of Eternal Light!

O' friends, wake up!
Give up this slumber.

Do not waste this precious life sleeping and squandering away your time.

I wish each one of you, my devotees, pick up the essence of this and meditate on it in your free time.

•••••

I reached Haridwar on an auspicious day of the holy Kumbh Mela. Thousands of people had gathered for a holy dip in the river Ganga. I wished to take bath in the holy river. The waters of the river Ganga it is said are pure and healing. No matter what garbage you throw into it, its waters remain pure and sacred. So I went up to the river bank and to my surprise I found people had little reverence for the holy river. They were spitting into the river. They were throwing garbage into the river. But the rushing waters of the Ganges swept away the dirt and the slush keeping the waters clean. The river, unmindful of the irreverence of the people flowed on showering benediction, on whoever came to it.

Before I could step into the river, 'Pandas', due to their greed, obstructed my way, and surrounded me. A few of them demanded money, others asked for a discourse to be delivered at their temples. I refused to concede to their irrelevant demands.

On that day, I took a vow that I would never visit a place of pilgrimage again. Rishis had done *'tapas'* on its banks. Those holy vibrations had disappeared due to human greed. The whole atmosphere had been vitiated by the aggressive behavior of the 'Pandas'.

I did take a dip in the river. It was an exhilarating experience. The waters of Ganges were cold and soothing and out of joy I called out, O' Mother Ganga, bless me!

•••••

One day I went to visit '*Swarg Ashram*'. It is a famous place in Haridwar. Many Sadhus and Sanyasis, from far and near visit this place to have Darshan, of the chief priest. In that ashram I met a Sindhi gentleman. He was very keen on taking me to a person who was a true devotee of the Lord. This man was a retired judge of the high court. He had renounced the worldly position, power, and wealth. He lived in a tiny room in the *Ashram*, living a simple life of a *Sadhak*. His humility came as a reminder for my own self. Let me be frank. My mind wavers and wanders and plays many monkey tricks. So after meeting him, I rebuked myself. I even wrote down a few lines of repentance.

> In temples you chime the bells ·
> On the flute you play the rhyme
> O' Shyam, O' Shyam!
> What have you achieved?
> Why don't you give up the chant of I? Give up your Ego and its pranks. Tell me. Be honest. What have you achieved?
> I question myself.
> O' open your eyes and wake up. Behold!
> View Shyam Sundar's beauty untold.
> He is friendly with the poor;
> He is smeared in mud and he shivers with cold.
> Shyam Sundar is the one to behold!
> He serves the poor. He is humble. An ocean of joy. He is the magician. He is the lover. He is the beloved. Shyam Sundar, Krishna is ecstasy manifold!

I reproach myself. Will Shyam accept me? I have still to fight many a battles. I have to erase the ego and be a dot, not even a zero. Unless I do this, Shyam Sundar will not accept me!

•••••

On my return from Dehradun I proceeded to Amritsar, to pay my respects at the Golden temple. I reached there at 4 am in the morning. The early dawn moon was bright, shining in the sky. A group of devotees had gathered and were immersed in singing *Naam Kirtan*. I was deeply moved by that sacred moment. I bowed down to the Divine Persona. And I heard a voice which has been singing in my ears ever since. Today that voice is shaped into words. Those words are a rich spiritual treasure. Those words are a mighty shake:

"My beloved, my Gurudev, my heart is ever in quest of you!
I am a prisoner wasting my days in anguish!
O' Fakir break these chains of attachment. Be free!
I peer at the sky and plead for your divine glimpse.
May I die in my native Malir!
May I be accepted by my Murshid.
My mind is filled with vicious thoughts. My heart is a river of sorrow. How can then I laugh?
I have lost my *splendor* committing sins.
And yet Nuri is all yours.
She knows no other way.
O' Gurudev you will be my *savior*, of that I am certain!"

••••

I went to Agra, as a guest at an acquaintance's house. There, one afternoon a group of English people came to meet me. They had come without an appointment but nevertheless I met them. I ask the English woman "What is it that I can do for you?" the English woman had a radiant face and a calm expression. Pulling out a book with a red cover, she handed it over to me. The book was titled 'Krishna the Savior'.

It so happened that she had learnt from the newspaper, that I was in town. She had read this book and was greatly moved by my book 'Krishna the *Savior*'. And therefore she had a keen desire to meet me. She pulls out a tiny book of Gita and says, "Look how I value these books. I always keep them by my bedside."

The word Krishna coming from this English woman cast a magic spell!

It brought tears to my eyes. In Germany and in Great Britain, I had met several people who had profound knowledge of the Gita and also had a unique faith in Sri Krishna.

•••••

The song of Gopis on the banks of the river Jamuna, has always been dear to me and by the grace of god, I today find myself on the banks of the river Jamuna. I was a guest in the house of an executive engineer. While talking to me, he revealed "I am delighted to have you here in this house. One day I will inscribe seven slokas on the walls of this building and I also wish," he did not complete the sentence but left it unsaid.

I asked him, "What do you wish?" He replied, "I wish to donate this whole building to you. I am not worthy of living in this house. I was in search of a Krishna *Bhakta*, who would deserve to live in this building, graciously sanctified by the chanting of mantras and prayers by *Bhaktas* of the Lord."

Several times during the day, I would chant the sweet name of Krishna. One night I move out of this building to be alone in solitude. I go and stand on the banks of the river Yamuna, watching the rythmic movement of waves. There in the dead silence of the dark night I speak to my beloved Krishna.

That night, the river Yamuna was swollen and the scene was frightening. Perhaps you do not know how awesome a swollen river looks.

Today, I am reminded of the day, I stood alone on the banks of the river Yamuna. Stormy winds blew and I was frightened. I may fall into its fast flowing current. I prayed to the lord, "I am alone but I have faith in your Divine protection."

There in that stormy weather in the solitude of the place I burst into a song.

'Yamuna Kinare.' It was a strange mystical experience, standing in the stormy weather on the banks of a flooded river.

Reverting back to that night I am engulfed by darkness. Everything appears eerie and scary. My eyes brim with tears as I yearn for Krishna. O Beloved. My dear Shyam, do not leave me, do not forget me, I call out.

One evening as I am sitting in the house of the Engineer, my heart cries out to *Shyam*; "I am unable to bear the agony of this separation. I long for you. When will you come and quench my thirst?"

And as I said this, I heard the echo of saint Mira's song. St Mira who was once a princess but became a roaming minstrel in search of her Lord. Mira sings: -

My heart belongs to my beloved.
I shall not live alone.
Now I have found the door of Raidas.
His knowledge I treasure more!

Mira is intoxicated by Love for the Lord. She finds this world worthless. She says, she's fortunate to have found her guru, a saintly soul, in Raidas. She has received *Gyan* (wisdom) from her Master.

She says, I roamed the desert in quest of you,
But now I rest at your shrine,
And get Divine blessings!
I am free from the cycle of birth and death.
Now I am one with you!

•••••

Many years ago I visited Delhi and was a guest in a rich man's house. He was a very wealthy man. He kept an open house and he entertained many guests. He was a perfect host. He would give a separate car and a servant to each of his guests. One day he came to my room and said, "I would like to show you around the house. I have accommodation for fifty guests. I have enough to give each of my guests a separate car and a separate servant."

One evening he took me for a long drive. We reached the brink of a forest. There he says: "lets sit down here for a while. I want to discuss something with you."

What does he discuss? "I am an unhappy man," he disclosed.

A man, who is spiritually poor, is bound to be unhappy. He may be rich in worldly wealth, but if his soul is starved of Divine food, then he is bound to be miserable. In Bhagavad Gita Arjuna says: if you want to be happy then cultivate your soul. In other words, grow within.

•••••

I was born in Hyderabad (Sind). The city had a very large *tikana* (prayer house). Many a times the trustees requested me to give discourses there. My discourse was based on the teachings of Guru Granth Sahib. I would pick a page from it and explain its meaning.

One day I come to know of a sad story of this beautiful worship place. I learn that the police had raided it; they broke open the place and forcibly entered the premises. This holy place had been foiled by an unpardonable sin.

Its *Mahant*, the chief priest was arrested. He was charged for committing the forbidden sin inside the sacred place. He was caught red-handed.

This incident saddened my heart for at that very place I had recited the sacred *'Gurbani'* and spoken of spiritual values. Unfortunately I found the same trend in many other temples also.

Our Sind had a very famous place of worship called *Sadhbelo*. Its *Mahant* was my friend; we had mutual respect for each other. I thought, with his help, I could bring about some changes in that place. One day the *Mahant Sahib* calls me up and requests me to visit him. He apprises me of the conference he wishes to hold. I ask him who will attend this conference and what was its purpose? He replied, "This is the conference of all the priests and *mahants*. I invite you to kindly inaugurate the conference."

"Me?" I ask, "I am too shy a person to inaugurate such a big conference. You do the honours." I request him instead. He agrees.

Many priests and heads of temples attend the conference. I reach the place an hour before the conference begins. I go around the temple to acquaint myself with the priest and to spread the message of *"Gurbani"*. As I go round, I notice that the priests have formed groups and are holding meetings in different rooms. By nature I trust people. Yet the behavior of these groups perturbs me. I peep into the rooms and I hear whispers. 'Making rounds, making rounds here he comes to catch us.' I hear, I wonder, what is up their sleeve? On a hunch I decide to enter one of the rooms and what I see is shocking, to say the least. I enquire of them, what is the matter? They snigger and snide. You are policing us, they accuse me. "Policing you?" I ask surprised. "Yes", then one of them pulls out a bottle of liquor and gives a bitter laugh. "We are drinking this," he says showing me the bottle, "and probably you are here to catch us." Alas! That is the sad state of many of our temples and places of worship. During my travels I have visited many temples and shrines and I have found them far from being clean and sacred.

•••••

June 4th of 1933 is a landmark day in my life. On this day, started the Mira movement in education. It was a sacred day. Early in the morning at 5 'o' clock we did the Havan, chanted mantras, read from the Bhagvat Gita and invoked the blessing of the Lord. We sat in silence and reflected. We read the Gita and prayed. The entire ambience was of peace and harmony.

I read out the sacred verses of saints, sages, and fakirs.

We also did a wonderful job of feeding the poor, because the saints of Indian culture and religions have said, "Service of poor is worship to the Lord."

I am sure they blessed that day, as well as the Mira movement in education. The day, these poor people will hoist the Mira flag, pray to Mira, invoke her blessings, and that day will be day of rejoicing for Mira. Because the aim of Mira education is to high light the truth, such as poor are the broken images of God. I hope that day is not far off when the students of Mira School will learn this important lesson of life and serve the poor as their own brothers and sisters. It is their blessings that will take the Mira movement forward, onward and Godward.

Many years ago I visited a town by the name of Bahawalpur. It was ruled by a Nawab. He was a Muslim, who had great reverence and sympathy for the Hindus. He believed in justice. The state should be ruled on the principal of justice, he said.

Bahawalpur had a college. And its principal invited me to address the students. The president of the college was the chief minister of that state. He was a Sindhi, and a very noble man. My talk to the students was, 'ideals of youth'. In my speech I emphasised the fact that this life is a trust. It was to be spent in the service of others.

The ideal life is one of sacrifice. Although most of the students were Muslims, they heard me keenly. I stayed for a few days more in Bahawalpur. There seemed some friction between Hindus and Muslims. I wanted to bridge the chasm between the two communities. I truly believe that there is One God. The same almighty takes care of both Hindus and Muslims. The almighty is called Allah the merciful one by the Muslims, and *daridranarayan*- the compassionate one by the Hindus. It was in this context that I desired to hold a meeting, where I could dispel their doubts and remove their misunderstanding. Many questions were asked at this meeting but I will discuss only a few of them here.

Q.1. You advised us to keep away from religious conflicts. We understand that Hindus and Muslims are part of one great humanity. Then please explain, why are there wars spurred by religion?

Ans.1 – This is so because; we do not understand the true meaning of our religion. Be it Hinduism, be it Islam, we only go by the words *Allah* or *Ishwar*. But we have never experienced either *Allah* or *Ishwar*. If we would experience (spirituality) we would not quarrel over the religion. Take the example of a honeybee. So long it is outside the flower, it buzzes. But once it gets inside and sucks the nectar it stops buzzing.

Similarly till we experience the spiritual nectar, we would bramble like bees, making noise about nothing.

Learn to drink the nectar of spiritualism. Do not quarrel over the superficial expression of the religion.

Q.2. – How to drink the heavenly nectar. Our minds are embedded in the religious differences right from birth?

Ans.2 – To taste the sweetness of heavenly nectar a few things are necessary:-

a) All conflict arises out of ignorance. Only if we would realise that we are the branches of the same tree.

b) Having understood oneness we should create love for others. There are many ways to realise God but every path preaches love for humanity.

Those who walk the way of love will reach the peak and meet the Lord.

Q.3. – How to cultivate this love?

Ans.3 – To open the floodgates of your hearts, it is necessary to get rid of your ego.

Love is the panacea for all ills.

Q.4 – What is the mark of such a love?

Ans.4 – A very good question.

The mark of love is neither words nor smile; it is your day-to-day living. Your everyday life should bear witness to the ideal of love. The mark of love is humility: Service of all in utter humility.

A man who truly loves is selfless. He does not bother about his looks and clothes. He is more concerned about the needs of others. Such a man is a true devotee for he serves not out of vanity but out of sheer love. It is said of Mohammad the Prophet that he did not care about his clothes or his food. His life was totally absorbed in service of the poor. One day while meeting the needs of others, he skipped his meal. When reminded to have his food, he said, "Give me a few dates and a tumbler of water."

This great prophet, the Beloved of God, could have asked for any food and his devotees would have been only too happy to serve him. But he had built his life in austerity, simplicity, purity and service of others.

Another Beloved of our hearts Sri Isha – Jesus Christ also lived a life of service and compassion.

It is said, that even before he opened his door, crowds gathered at his house. Ill, diseased, starved and hungry crowds thronged him seeking help, love, and medicine. Our Beloved Jesus would then dispense medicine, clothes and food to the needy. Taking their blessings he would move out to the town, with the words: Give, Give, Give.

Learn to Give. Hindus and Muslims, learn to Give. Give sympathy, Give love, Give help, Give blessings, Give service, Give affection and make your life worthy of God's benediction.

•••••

Many years ago. I happened to be in a small village. There, I was delighted to see that Janmashtmi was celebrated with great enthusiasm. Funfair and joy rides etc. In that joyful atmosphere I could hear someone playing on a flute. I said to myself: how beautifully have these innocent villagers totally immersed themselves in the music of Shyam.

•••••

I am a great lover of trees. Even as a student I spent quite sometime under the trees. In Sanskrit tree is called '*Vruksh*', which means protection. Another root of this word *Vruksh* is '*brayha*' which means growth. Tree is the symbol of life. Its message is to give and give. May we take this lesson from the tree.

When I visited Buddha Gaya I had the privilege to see the great Bodhi tree. This is a place of Pilgrimage and people from all over the world come to pay their respects to this sacred tree. Among the many visitors present there were Prince and Princess of Nepal, they bowed at the tree with great reverence every now and then. There were Lamas from Tibetan monasteries. I learnt that one of them had observed silence for a number of years. Strange enough, even such a holy person had come to pay his respects to the Bodhi tree.

Another great tree, which has influenced my life, is the tree in Nurela Mountains in Sri Lanka. I visited the '*Ashoka Ban*' where Sita had been kept in captivity by the demon King Ravana. It is here in *Ashokaban*, that Sita spent her days in prayers, austerity and *tapasya*/penance. After I spent sometime in *Ashokaban* I asked myself, what do these trees teach us? Every tree speaks:

1) **I am tolerant.** I tolerate the heat of the sun. I tolerate the down pour of the rain. I bear the pain in silence. I never complain.

2) **I provide protection.** I protect the travellers from the heat. I give them shade. I protect them from rain. I give them cover.

   How many of us provide the protection to others?

3) **I stand straight. I grow upwards.**

How many of us grow upwards? How many of us look upon the radiance of the Sun? Whenever you feel low and depressed, then look up to the radiance of the angels in the sky.

4) **I give fruit to one and all.**

May we learn this lesson and spend our life in the service of the poor and forlorn. For the joy of life lies in Service.

I was in Lucknow and a gentleman takes me to see a temple. I asked him, who has built this beautiful temple and how much he has spent on it? The gentleman replied, "A wealthy businessman has built this temple. He is no more. He did not wish to be known. He made a request to keep his name a secret and not to inscribe it anywhere in the temple. As far as the expenditure of the temple is concerned it has come from the Lord Almighty."

My dear *Satsangis* you should give in charity unsung without any claim to name and fame. All that we have is a loan given to us and it should be spent in the service of the others.

When man is devoid of ego, then this Spiritual quest deepens.

With all the longing and yearning call out

O' Lord let me have a glimpse of thee.

Accept me at thy holy feet!

I also visited Kanpur, to attend the celebrations being held in the sacred memory of Sri Ramakrishna Parmahansa.

Once Sri Ramakrishna Parmahansa was asked "Swamiji, which is the easiest spiritual path to realise God?"

Sri Ramakrishna replied, "Call out to the Mother Divine, call out to her with all the yearning. She will surely answer your call." May you also thirst for the Mother Divine and pray to her to show the light in this dark desert of life.

I was once invited to the city of Udaipur; I stayed there for a few days. Just before I was leaving, a suggestion came to me, to visit a temple, which lies, on the way from Udaipur to Sind. In this temple I was told, milk flows like a river. Everyday devotees bring a glass of milk and pour it on the idol. In this temple food is cooked and puris fried which is available for 4 annas and 8 annas according to the choice of devotees. The temple receives groceries at a cheap rate and they make money on it. I felt sad at this mundane state of the temple. The food is not dedicated to the God but is sold commercially. The temples are collecting gold and becoming rich when thousands of people are poor and starving.

The *Mahant* of this temple had a son of marriageable age. The son was keen to get married and wanted father's permission to do so.

The Mahant replied, "Yes son I'll get you married at the proper time."

To which the son answered, "But father, I want to get married to a girl of my own choice."

The father did not mind it but when he is told that the girl is a Muslim, he is put into a dilemma. Ultimately he finds the solution in separating his son from the household.

"Take this one lakh of rupees and build your own house and marry the girl of your own choice. I am the head priest. I cannot get you married to a Muslim girl," he tells his son.

Imagine a *Mahant* the caretaker of the temple, was able to give his son a lakh of rupees, a stupendous sum in those days. How disgraceful that money which is an offering of the devotees to their temple of worship is used for personal purpose. *Mahant* was just a trustee to use this money for the welfare of the people and not for his own selfish ends.

•••••

Mira was a spiritual genius. She gave up a life of luxury for the sake of her beloved Shyam.

Perhaps many of you do not know what a life of luxury is. I have a first hand knowledge of a life in a palace. For a few days I was a guest of a queen. I was surprised to see so many comforts and luxuries provided there. The food was sumptuous, with cereals, vegetables, fruits and a variety of delicious desserts. I used to get a tray of food, which could easily feed 12 persons. The life inside a palace is lavish but Mira a princess leaves the lavish living of the palace in the quest of her beloved Shyam.

One evening sitting alone in a corner of the palace I reflected on Mira. How could anyone living in such an abundant luxury, ever be spiritual? I ask myself again and again. More so, because every time I rang the bell, a host of servants rushed in Hukum! Hukum! How could Mira abandon such pleasures for her spiritual quest?

These are my thoughts as I climb the rocky steps that lead to the palace of princess of Mewar in Chitor. I reflect: Mira must have descended from these very steps, which I am climbing now as a pilgrim. At the top where the palace is, Mira had built a temple for her Krishna. I imagined Mira going down the stone steps, leaving behind her royalty and going in search of Krishna. 'I seek only Krishna. For me there is none other', she cries.

I recollect here an incident that happened in my life.

I was in Sind and for a few days I was housed in a jail. The jailor was an Irish man. He was not only a pleasant person but also a very kind one. It was the rule of the jail to lock the prison cells in the night and open them again in the morning. When the Irish jailor learnt of me, he ordered the authorities not to lock me up in the night, because I would not run away even when given a chance.

It was my routine to begin the day with recitation from the Bhagavad Gita. One day after the Gita recitation I was sitting in silence, when a man came and stood before me. From his dress and built he appeared to be a Muslim. I enquired of him about his wellbeing and asked him why he was put into jail. The man confessed that he had committed an unforgivable crime, so he was imprisoned. Repentant, in a heavy voice, he says, "I have heard that you are a *Darvesh* and so I have come to you to seek forgiveness." He pleads for forgiveness again and again.

"What is your crime, my dear and why do you seek forgiveness from me? Please, ask the Almighty God to pardon you. He alone can forgive your sins". This repentant prisoner discloses the crime he has committed. "One day in my anger I picked up an axe and killed a man. I just cut his head with the axe. Immediately I was arrested and given life imprisonment." Hearing this I asked him, if he had any formal education.

> "I am uneducated, I have learnt nothing, and I know only the name of Allah. In this prison cell, I keep crying out to the Almighty for forgiveness. You are a *Darvesh* and a *Fakir*. You can forgive me and atone my sins."

I looked into his face and saw his tears of true repentance. I was touched.

Yet, another incidence comes to my mind. During the summer months, Hyderabad would get very hot. I could go out for a stroll only late in the evening. I normally walked on *Takri* which is close to the jail. One evening on my way back I came across a few prisoners in chains. I entered into conversation with them, comforting them with a few affectionate words. Touched, one of the prisoners said with a twinkle in his eye, "Thank God, I am not alone in this world. At least there is one soul who thinks I am worth talking to". Just then the prisoners were ordered to turn around and return to the jail. The other prisoners also wanted to talk to me but their outdoor time was up. They kept turning back, glancing at me and saying,, *'Khudah Haffis'*. May the Almighty bless you. I began to think, may be in this dry desert of life, there are many who are lonely and forlorn, yearning for a word of comfort and kindness.

Why does anyone commit a crime? I ask myself. Why do people turn criminals? Is it because they live in poverty and suffer deprivation? Who is ultimately responsible for their crimes? Are we not too, thieves? Don't we amass wealth? Don't we deprive others of their basic necessities? Don't we lock up our money? Aren't we too criminals? These and many such thoughts flashed through my mind and I at once felt sorry for the criminals who had been chained and put behind the bars. I wish we could close down the prisons and turn these places into schools and *satsangs*, which would teach values of sharing and caring. Merely to punish the criminal is not the solution. An eye for an eye and a tooth for a tooth would make every one blind. What is needed is to impart the right values and bring about a change in the hearts of people, to replace hate by love, and fear by faith.

•••••

I met Mahatma Gandhi in Sind. He had come there to tour the villages and to find out the level of poverty and misery of the rural people. The first time Mahatma Gandhi visited Sind, he was a guest in a friend's house in Karachi. I went to visit him there, and found him sitting alone in silence in a corner of a room. One look at him and I knew how much he cared for poverty stricken people of India.

Years later, Gandhi came to Karachi. A public meeting was organised at Idgah grounds. His train was late and therefore he was very tired. He pleaded to be excused but the enthusiastic public would not allow him to go. He made a brief speech. 'My dear fellow beings of Bharat. I have but one word to say. Be soldiers. Uphold the honour of your country!' Those moving words touched me. He had immense love for his countrymen.

Mahatma Gandhi was to leave for Hyderabad the next morning. He sent me a message, requesting me to go with him, because Hyderabad was my hometown. I packed up quickly and left for Hyderabad with Gandhiji.

I had the rare privilege of meeting Gandhiji personally. During our meeting he requested me to attend the conference organised for him in Hyderabad. Why all this formality? I asked Gandhiji 'Because you are a shy introvert person,' he replied.

The next visit on his itinerary was Rohri. Once again Gandhiji requested me to accompany him to this sacred place. Gandhiji never dictated terms. He only made humble requests. The only two rules he imposed with great authority were, one, wear Khadi and two, spin the spinning wheel.

After I had breakfast at Sukkar, (where I lived then) I went out with Gandhiji for a stroll on the bridge. There was another gentleman accompanying us. He begs of Gandhiji to be allowed to ask a question and Gandhiji readily agrees.

"All these meetings, lectures, speeches are futile exercise. I need freedom, inner freedom, I want 'Mukti'. Kindly show me the true path to this 'freedom of the soul!'"

Gandhiji fell into silence. He was a man of silence and of sweet smile. For a minute or two, he remained in that silence, before replying, 'I do not know of the path that leads to the liberation of soul or what you term as 'Mukti'. I can but tell you of my own experiences. My experience has been, that the road to true freedom lies in Service; service of the poor is the true worship of the Lord!'

Hearing those words, tears rolled down my eyes. Surely, the gentleman who asked for the path of True Freedom, was also equally moved by Gandhiji's words. For Gandhiji said, 'Go about your daily routine work. But remember, the true work is service to others.'

The same message has come to me through an invisible source. This happened when I was staying in Simla. During the summer, the region I belong to, would be like a big furnace. To escape the sizzling heat I used to spend summers at Simla. One morning in Simla, I found queues of people, all rushing and pushing ahead. On enquiry, I found that a Sadhu who lived in a cave in the Shivalik hills had come. This Sadhu ate his meals very early.

Each one in that long queue of people had brought meals for him. Each wanted to be the first one and be blessed by the Sadhu. The Sadhu came out of his cave, he accepted the food from a person at the head of the queue, then he retreated into his cave again. But before he left, he blessed the people 'God bless you. May you be happy. But true happiness lies in the service of the broken ones.'

May you, my dear ones, carry this message in your heart. True freedom will come only when the poor are free from poverty.

Want to be happy? Then serve others and make them feel happy!

•••••

In Colombo.

A friend, who is a doctor, came to visit me. He did not like the look on my face. He felt I had become pale and needed a change of place. He advised sea travel and asked me to go to Colombo. 'The sea rejuvenates you. You like to travel by sea!' He said with conviction. He recommended a place called Neuwara near Colombo, in Sri Lanka (then it was called Ceylon).

Truly, the leisurely travel by the sea envigorated me. When I had travelled to England, many years ago, I had enjoyed it and gained health and also weight!

I realised that I needed a holiday and a change of place to feel fit. So we started on our journey. We were a group of five. On reaching Colombo we met many Sindhis who lived there. They showered love and affection on us and indeed took very good care of us. Colombo excited me. It brought alive the panorama of Ram, Sita, Laxman and their devotee Hanuman. Even now, as the festival of Dashera nears, my thoughts move out to them.

I went to South India, to Madras, before proceeding to Lanka. On the day of Diwali, I was taken to a village. We went there by a small boat, every boat was lit with lamps; tiny lamps floated on the water. We went to a village which was celebrating Diwali. Every house was lit with a lamp. The whole village was illuminated - there is light, there is brilliance, but the people are very poor. They are of ill health, wearing skimpy clothes- tattered-some were naked. I was shocked at their dire conditions, yet these very poor people, received me with grace and dignity. I was glad I visited that village as I had a glimpse of the poverty prevalent in our villages in India.

The villagers looked grim with grief; there was no joy on their faces; yet with love and affection they sing a song for me. The song of pathos and pain. The song, which I am able to recollect in parts.

I wonder, how these poor, poverty-ridden villagers living in want and starvation, can sing a beautiful song? My heart- bursts into words of sorrow:

It runs – Oh God, how can you bear to see your children, naked and starving?

Oh Lord, how can you witness this sorrow and not be moved?

These words disturbed me again and again. I called for the brother who handles our 'Service' (Seva) department. I requested him, to send clothes to the naked and food to the hungry. Further I asked him to send clothes and food in plenty, so that every one who is naked is clothed decently; every one who is hungry gets plenty to eat. This Diwali, let these villagers of the coast of Madras, have enough of food and clothing.

Do you know what song they were singing?
The song is,

The King Ram will come!
He will come to wipe our tears,
He will come to bless us, the poor.

This song brings hope; the song brings confidence; the song brings security and the positive thought that Ram will surely come and end their misery.

May we also have faith in these words. May we believe that Ram the harbinger of hope and happiness will come and bless us with his benign look.

In Sri Lanka, I had the opportunity to go to the mountains. I find many *viharas*, where the Buddhist *Bhikhus* live. Buddhism is still a powerful religion in Sri Lanka. These *Bhikhus* live an austere life, rotating rosary beads with the chant, *Buddham Sharanam Ghachami*. I visited *viharas*, I visited temples. Everywhere I heard the sacred chants of Buddha. Austerity, devotion and compassion best describe the Buddhist monks and *Bhikhus*. They are humble, gentle. All they ask me is to put a flower at the lotus feet of *Lord Buddha*!

I went to meet a few *Bhikhus*. What I saw amazed me. Wrapped in silence, they sit in quietitude, murmuring *Buddham Sharanam Gachchami*. The whole environment is sacred and purifying.

On the other hand, what is the condition of our temples? Untold quantities of *gold* and *silver* are locked in the temple chests. I would suggest break those money boxes and secret vaults containing gold and spend that money in the service of the poor; give clothes and food to the poverty stricken people; bring them medicines.

Compare our temples with the '*Viharas*'. Every monk brings a flower and places it at the holy feet of the Lord with the words *Buddham Sharanam Gachchami*.

Gautam Buddha is highly revered in Sri Lanka. In his memory, a procession is taken out, similar to the one we have for Guru Nanak Dev. But the procession here moves in silence. The chant of *Buddham Sharanam Gachchami* is a whisper. There is no noise, no slogans, no cry, but a silent procession evoking peace and bliss.

Gautam the Buddha was born in India; he attained Nirvana in India, but he is forgotten in India. In Ceylon, in the Far East, Gautam the Buddha is revered and worshipped with great devotion and emotion. May we in India, revive our love and our reverence for this great soul of India.

Long ago, I visited Buddh Gaya. I took the blessings of the tree called Buddha *Vurksh*. There I saw something remarkable. The prince and his queen and other members of Nepal Royal family were circumbulating the sacred tree, three times, in silence. Their devotion, their reverence, their silent murmuring of chants left an indelible mark on my mind. Their deep devotion moved me deeply.

It is said, Gautam the Buddha, went to Gaya, near Banaras. There, when he comes out of his silence, he speaks words, which are pearls of wisdom. Devotees then ask him, 'Give us your teachings'. Buddha gives them his teachings.

The first teaching is: Look Oh dear ones! Open your eyes. Watch. The world is full of sorrow. The Kings, the

Monarchs, the Villagers all are filled with grief. There is pain everywhere.

I recall, in the U.S.A an affluent man, rolling in wealth, committed suicide. He was unhappy, and a disturbed man. In his suicide note he wrote: the world is full of sorrow. There is pain and unbearable suffering. I am unable to live in this world!

I recount a similar incident. Once I was invited by the queen of a well-known state to be her houseguest for a few days. The queen meets me and opens her heart. 'I am miserable! I have everything a woman can ask for – servants, mansions, luxuries, silks and diamonds, yet I am unhappy.'

I was her guest for twelve days. I was served the choicest food. Yet, her words haunted me. *What is the cause of my unhappiness?*

Years ago, I was in Lahore. There too, I was invited by a princess to a dinner at the royal palace.

The queen had expressed her desire to meet me. Hence the dinner. The queen was well educated and spoke in English. She had love for *'Satsang'*. But she said, 'My dear brother, please tell me, what is the root cause of all suffering?'

True was the saying of Buddha: wherever you look, there is suffering.

Gautam retreats in silence, silence was his hallmark, in silence he replies-

'The root cause of all suffering is desire.'

The devotees ask, 'What is this desire?'

Buddha replies, 'Sit in silence, and I will reveal to you The Great Laws.

The first law is desire. Desire burns you in the fire of hell.

The second law is *Nirvana*. *Nirvana* releases you from the throes of suffering. You are liberated. For *Nirvana* is a state of zero desire.

Desires, ambition, ego, should be erased to achieve that blissful state. The fire of worldly attachment can be doused with the annihilation of desire. Be nothing and enter the Blissful state of *Nirvana*.'

I must tell you of Guru Nanak Dev's words, which are similar- ***'I am nothing Oh Lord! Thou are my all!***

One day as I was returning from my walk in Neuwara, I met a British woman. She was an elderly Christian lady. She asked me a question, **What is your religion**?

Answer: My religion is every religion.

Question: How can that be? Only one religion is true.

Answer: All religions convey the same truth.

Question: Only one religion is true – Christianity. All other religions are hocus-pocus.

Answer: Look at this garden. It has so many flowers of different kind. Every flower is beautiful in its own way. Each flower has its own fragrance.

(Sri Krishna has said, all religions are mine. For on all the paths I see the splendour of Shyam.)

On my way back to India from Srilanka, I visited Rameshwaram. It is a place of pilgrimage. I took a dip into a pond, and as I was returning, a group of children followed me. Among them was a saffron robed *sanyasi*. Although, he was wearing a *Sanyasis* colour, he had not truly renounced the world. He appeared to be greedy and ambitious. True Renunciation is of the mind. True renunciation is *Shakti*. Renunciation is tyag which comes with the knowledge that this world is an illusion. This world is nothing. *Vairag* means to shun the Untruth/ unreality and accept the Truth/the reality. One who gains this awareness is on the right path of spirituality.

After my bath in the pond, I went to the temple. The '*Pandit*', the priest of the temple was performing pooja. He asked me to put one rupee in the worship plate. I wondered why one rupee, why not one 'anna'? I smiled at the priest. But he insisted that I put one rupee. There on I quoted in Sanskrit the sloka from Bhagavad Gita: one leaf, one flower, one fruit, and a sprinkle of water given with devotion is all I ask. Hearing this, the priest became furious. Such was his anger, that he threw the worship plate (*aarti*) into my face.

I smiled and paying my respects to Sri Rama I hastened to go out.

What kind of temples are these?

May be the religious culture of south India is different. Once, I visited Sri Sankacharaya's temple. There a priest asked me, if I wished to go inside the temple. I was tempted. I went with him. He came up to the threshold and then said "To enter the sanctum and to have '*Darshan*' of Ram, you pay me one rupee." To pay one rupee, for the *darshan* of Sri Ram in his own temple? The idea did not go well with me. In fact I was disturbed. What greed of the temple people. I prayed that Sri Ram may have mercy and shower his kindness so that we may be able to live up to his holy name.

It was years ago that I went down to south. It was an invitation to address a meeting in Madras. In those days, I was young and energetic. I could speak without microphone. My voice was loud enough to be heard across those huge halls! Now, my voice is soft and weak. Perhaps it is so because of my sorrow, my pain, and my eternal quest.

In Madras, before I began my speech, a brother puts me a question: "we have heard about you, read about you, even listened to your discourses and speeches, and yet, we do not know much about you. Who are you? Kindly tell us about yourself and the purpose of your discourse here?"

I bow down to the audience humbly. I begin my speech as – 'Dear brothers and sisters. I am a farmer. I am a peasant. I have come here to sow the seeds.'

Today, I remind myself of those words, words which are the gift of wisdom, from our *fakir* and *darvesh* poet. A poet, whose greatness will be revealed to the world. I hope it will happen soon. A poet, whose poetry is beyond description, whose thought is beyond mundane world, whose diction is rich with alliteration. Such a poet has given us a language which is the rich treasure of Sindhis. Perhaps, no one knows, the beauty, the depth, the dimension of this heritage, which belongs not only to Sind, but to the whole of India. Truly, Sindhi language is the richest language of the world!

That great poet par excellence wails:
Oh living in Maleer, What have I achieved!

I have been in these beautiful surroundings of Maleer, and yet whiled away my time.

I am a peasant, I am a farmer, and what have I done? Have I ploughed the fields? Have I sowed the seeds? Pondering over these thoughts, I shed tears of repentance! Reflecting on my life, I shudder to think of the time wasted. God has been ever kind and ever loving. Yet, what have I achieved? As a farmer, have I succeeded in my mission? One thing I am aware of! Many a times I have kept God aside; many a times I have been amidst saints and sages, but have kept a distance from them. But believe me I have been aware of One truth, that is, this world is not my home. My native place is elsewhere! It is this one thought that has been the pillar of my life. My happiness, my joy is not among the pleasures of the world. My home, my happiness, lies elsewhere!

This truth, this Awareness, is itself the Grace of my Lord, my Master! I have deeply reflected on this thought and made it a watch dog of my life.

My home is not here! My home is at Thy lotus feet! Bless me!

This thought is firmly ingrained in my mind. It is with this awareness, that I wrote this song which when loosely translated from Sindhi, runs as,

You are a farmer in His field of Truth,
You have to plough His fields...
No one can destroy your crop, your efforts,
For it has the protection of me.
O Awake Sentinel- Guard your fields!
Be in the world as a witness, ever remembering
His Holy name.
Sentinel of spirituality,
Drink this wine and offer it to others,
Work with your hands, but keep your heart intact.

Sow the seeds of love, in these fields, today,
Oh Nuri, may the smiling Shyam Sunder Bless.

Awake, sow the seeds now, today!

•••••

I have been impressed by Madan Mohan Malaviya, that stalwart of India, who established the Benaras Hindu University. One of the interesting features of this University, is a touch of spirituality, through the study of Bhagavad Gita.

Madan Mohan Malaviya had great fondness for Bhagavad Gita; he thought its study would contribute to the Indian culture of Sri Krishna.

I met Madan Mohan Malaviya in his small house on the large sprawling campus of this great University. Students thronged outside his house, creating much noise. Amidst that hustle bustle, lived the great son of the soil. He was frail; and weak of health. He was to preside over my lecture, but due to indisposition of his health, he could not do so. When I visited him, I found him chanting the name of the Lord. Although his body was weak, his spirit was strong.

We discussed Bhagavad Gita. He had already received the copy of my speech in Calcutta, which had the theme of Gita. He was thrilled to read it. Madan Mohan Malaviya waxed eloquence, and talked continuously. His face had a child like look, but his mind had the wisdom of a *Rishi*. He said, let's be strong as the characters of Mahabharat. Lets imbibe the virtues of Arjun and Yudishtra and Bhisham Pitamha. Let's be strong and courageous and not be mere weaklings- or else we will be trampled.

Madan Mohan Malviya had a soft spot for Sindhis and Sind.

•••••

This reminds me of Shah Abdul Latif. Shah Abdul Latif went to a desert place called Bhit. Bhit means a 'mound of sand' (sand dune). There he formed a group and created a small hamlet. The hamlet came to be called Bhit.

I go to Bhit, to pay my respects to this Great Sufi seer poet. I wish to acknowledge his greatness, his mystical Sufism, his vedantic poetry. I go there with beloved Jashan. We reached Hala, the nearest rail head at 7 pm in the evening. It had rained. We had to travel by tonga for two hours or so, to reach Bhit. It was already dark and cloudy. We could not get any transport. The tongawalla said, it is dangerous to travel at this hour. We have to go through a desolate area, through jungles and arid region. There is no light and the area is infested by dacoits and thugs. Life was dear to him as it is to everyone.

I told Jashan, 'We must go today. Because today is Friday. It is the night of Vigil.' I did not wish to wait till the next Friday night. I said so to beloved Jashan. While we were debating how to reach Bhit, one tongewalla came up and agreed to take us there. But after talking to this other tongewalla, he changed his mind. 'I can take you by another road which is longer.' Doesn't matter, I told him.' It was a lonely, desolate road. Not a soul was in sight. The night was dark. We galloped on the uneven path. Beloved Jashan said, 'Do not crane your neck out; do not look outside. I will handle them (dacoits) if they come'. He was really concerned about me.

'Dear Jashan,' I said, 'God is our protector. He is our guardian. He will take care of everything.'

When we approached Bhit, the dogs started barking and howling. We detoured and reached Bhit. Surprisingly, there were 700, 800, 900 or 1000 people, gathered there to pay their homage to Sufi Shah Latif. Peasants, farmers, farm hands, labourers and small traders had gathered in devotion and love, paying their respects to the Sufi mystic. That scene is unforgettable. It has remained a pleasant memory with me. We mingled with the crowds of spirituals and prayed at the *'dargah'* of the saint.

The morning gave us a clearer picture of Bhit. It had tea stalls, where people were having tea. It hurt me, to see commercialisation making inroads into this small spiritual hamlet- hamlet built by Shah Abdul Latif after hard struggle, of fetching water from far, and growing trees. For today the place has large beautiful trees along the sand dune. Shah Latif with his magical mind had created an oasis in the desert.

We visited the tomb, where a few relics of Shah are still kept. His turban, his stick, his robe etc, there I met a man, a descendent of Shah's family, a 'sayeed'. He said, he doesn't want the 'gaddi' (throne). He relinquished it in favour of his younger brother. An image of simplicity, he sat there in front of the tomb, wrapped in silence and praying. We bowed to him, and sought his blessings!

•••••

30th January 1948. I was in Hyderabad Sind. I received the news of the tragic death of our beloved Mahatma Gandhi. I went into silence. I consoled myself with the words – Oh man, don't mourn the death, but in silence, listen to the voice: open the Lotus of your heart.

I went into deep silence. What did I hear?

There is no death for those who live for others,

They are the ones who breath the spiritual breath!

Mahatma Gandhi knew the true purpose of our life, here on this earth. He knew that Service is the true aim of life. He had also spiritual aspirations. He knew that soul is immortal and ever living! Life hides death; and death hides life!

Krishna did not die!

Guru Nanak did not die! Gautam the Buddha, Chaitanya Mahaprabhu- none of them died. They live on forever, here as well as there. Gandhi is not dead. Gandhi is alive. He is ever living. There is no death for such souls, humble, committed, austere and devoted to the cause of people, freedom, and humanity. I bow down to this great man of *Ahimsa*, peace and love; the man called **Mahatma Gandhi.**

Who was Mahatma Gandhi? Many call him father of the Nation. He had sacrificed his whole life for the freedom of the nation. Another beloved son of Bharat, Lokmanya Tilak, also sacrificed his life for the country. Subash Chandra Bose also travelled far and wide, to gather support for the freedom of the country; he gave up his life for the unity and freedom of his motherland.

India became a free country. Mahatma Gandhi became the father of free India. I have a picture of Mahatma in my mind: Mahatma who was a friend of all; a brother of all, comforter of all. He truly was a 'brother' to every one, rich and poor, the suppressed and the exploited.

Do you know what the real meaning of 'brother' is? 'Brother' means *'bradar'*, which means burden bearer. Gandhi was a brother to millions of people. At one place Gandhiji has written:

'Even if my body is cut into pieces

I should not be away from my suffering people.'

May we all imbibe this lofty message of brother-hood. Time and again, Gandhiji implored people, 'Do not quarrel over religion. We all are brothers and sisters!'

Gujaratis, Maharastrians, Madrasis, Bengalis, and Sindhis, Punjabis, are children of the same soil. 'You are brothers and sisters. Therefore support one another.'

Today, millions are plunged into sorrow. We have left behind our sun-lit Sind, our rich heritage, our cultural treasures, we have left behind our homes, our wealth, our fields, our houses, our everything. We have migrated to India, leaving behind our ancestral homes and properties.

All the more reason, we should live together as brothers and sisters; we should hold the community together. May we provide support to one another, may we care and share our sorrows and joys together.

I wish, there comes a leader like Mahatma Gandhi, who would give the clarion call of unity and love.

Mahatma Gandhi sacrificed, suffered and became a martyr. His life was a *'Yagna'*. He suffered physically; he tortured himself with austerity and frugal living. Why? So that we could identify ourselves with the poverty stricken mass; starving masses; naked masses.

Gandhiji gave the world, our ancient mantra, our message of Rishis and wise men; the mantra of Ahimsa: Peace without quarrel or bloodshed.

[There are two paths I said to myself. One is of love and the other of evil. The evil is of five vices: *kam, krodh, lobh, moh* and *ahankar*. i.e. lust, anger, violence, greed, attachment and ego.]

When Gandhiji visited Sind, the students of Karachi College, ridiculed him. This man? Who is he? But Gandhi proved that humility, and *Ahimsa* can shake the mighty British Empire, because Gandhiji represented millions of Indians and their aspirations. May God ever bless his soul!

After the Partition in India

Hyderabad Sind. The city of saints and fakirs. The city on the banks of that great river Indus; Indus that flows eternally- the river whose banks are celebrated as the seat of wisdom; the wisdom that is of Vedas, so beautifully written on these banks. Indus river, from which India gets its name and fame. That river, which reverberates with *Sufi kalaams*.

In that Hyderabad city, on a quiet night, in the solitude of my heart, a question arises: 'Should I leave? Should I go?' Should I leave my Sind, my beautiful sun-lit Sind; Sind with which I am bonded immortally With heavy heart and tears in my eyes, I ask myself the pertinent question: should I leave my beloved Sind? That night I wept tears of sorrow.

Then I heard a voice, which urged me to go; across the border and spread the spiritual light in the newly created India. Sind now belongs to Pakistan, which was created on religious ground. 'Go to free India, experience its joys, its sorrow, serve those who are in pain, and poverty.' I realised that the spiritual light of our saints and sages, was receding; and darkness of evil was casting its shadow on my beloved Sind. Temples were destroyed; Hindu shrines grazed to ground, our holy places were being desecrated. It was a painful scenario. Our ancient culture of peace and harmony was being trashed. I heard a faint whisper of Sufis. Was it all a dream or a reality?

In India, I find myself as a refugee. No. I am a pilgrim. I must move on. My real home, my true Native place is elsewhere. My home is in the land of service. Dark energies have engulfed the sub-continent. And a Sindhi is the worst victim of that. These dark energies are demolishing temples and shrines which were built with the sacrifices made by people. These evil energies can destroy the physicality of Sind; but its spiritual treasure of Shah and Sami, its Sufi songs and *kalaams* of *darveshes*, its spiritual wisdom will last for ever, for it is beyond physical destruction.

I visit a home of a dear Satsangi. He is on the last stage of his earthly journey. By the Grace of God, he has everything, but now at this fag end of his life, he is helpless on the bed. He was a devotee, who came regularly to Satsang. Once he sent me four hundred rupees with the request not to disclose his identity.

That is the mark of a person who is spiritually awakened. He knows the value of *'Gupt daan'* (secret donation). This devotee was a blessed man. I implore you, my fellow beings, earn your blessings. Chant the name of God, and do service to society. Life is fleeting, the end is certain, do not waste more time, but earn the blessings, chant the name of the Lord. It is this 'Spiritual Growth' that you will carry to the other shore. It is this wealth of spiritual assets that will transcend the death and accompany you. My dear ones, waste no more time, chant and chant, give and give and you will be happy.

A saint has said,

'You did not bargain, when the bazaar was open.'

'O foolish man! You did not strike a deal when the sale was on. The saints have often given a call. Come and take away the key to the life beautiful. Spiritual goods are available in plenty with us. But you did not heed the call. Now on the deathbed you regret. You did not avail of the golden opportunity. You missed out on the real deal.

Oh foolish man! Now when the bazaar is closed you think of the lost deal'

Come to think of it. You never did go to the Bazaar. You never did buy your spiritual kit.

Hope you realise the need for the spiritual kit and buy it in time. Lest you repent and weep.

One day, I am inside my room with doors and windows shut. For some reason I feel suffocated. I wish to go out to bazaar and watch the people shop. I send a word to beloved Jashan. He comes immediately. "Jashan dear, I wish to go to the bazaar," I tell him. He agrees, and we go out into the buzz of activity, that is the bazaar. I watch the people and the shopkeepers, and feel sad. My visit to the bazaar was impromptu and I instructed Jashan not to inform anyone about my visit. In spite of that, someone in the crowd recognized me, and calls out, 'Vaswani, Vaswani'. This man was educated, but little; he pleaded with me, to say a few words. I was hesitant. I wanted to visit the bazaar unobtrusively, without anyone knowing about it. Yet, this man persists. His sincerity makes me say, 'Don't go empty handed from this world'. We all have to go from here. Where to, I don't know, but we have to move on. We should carry with us something. What is that something? Blessings of the poor and needy? Blessings of the sick and the forlorn?

Long ago, I had read about a saint, who made it a point to meet people, speak to them, deliver discourses. Even when he was tired, he would continue his dialogue with the people. When he was exhausted, he would go to a water hole, and sit by its side, in silence.

Rejuvenated by the silence and meditation, he would again embark on his mission, and talk to the people, give them comfort, and serve them in every way.

One night, I found myself in Dr. Coyaji Home (Pune). Perhaps, in the middle of the night, I was shifted to the Dr. Coyaji Home. I remained there for many days. I felt, I was by the side of a well brimming with water; which I was drinking in silence. Dr. Coyaji Home was like a retreat for me. My stay there was a rejuvenating experience.

Days passed by. I spent my time in silence, calling out to the Lord: Liberate me, Liberate my soul. Ill of health, lying on bed, in Coyaji Home, my heart aspired for freedom: I prayed,

Oh Lord, let me be free as a bird in the sky. Let my soul soar and be free like the clouds in the sky. Let me feel the joy of freedom, the joy of the rainbow sky.

Break my bonds; break my chains. Liberate me O Lord!

Lying on the bed, ill of health, I heard a voice, a whisper which echoed again and again in my ears.

Awake! Awake! Awake!

Who is free? Who is liberated? The one who is awake!

Awake! Do not slumber. See the Light.

This song stayed with me at Coyaji Home. During my illness, I realised God's Grace; and his infinite kindness and mercy! There is a message in whatever happens.

Sami – the Sufi poet - has, in one of his slokas said:

How am I to acknowledge the Mercy of God,

How am I to applaud his Grace?

It is like the cloud burst, which beautifies everything on the earth.

Although my body suffered pain, my heart was full of joy; I felt the spring in my heart. Seeing this magic of His Mercy, I wrote,

The spirit bounces with joy,

For, it has seen the rejuvenation of this body.

Physical suffering purifies the soul. During my delirious state, I had strange experiences. Once, I felt that I had travelled to the other shore. But alas, I am refused entry. There is no place for you here, I heard voices. In that condition, I penned a few lines,

You are dear to me,

Break all attachments, all that is illusion.

Go back, go back, to your mud house,

And beg Almighty of his grace!

I have returned to you my devotees, as a child, devoid of chains of the attachment. I behave like a child, and speak like a child. I bow down to you, and ask you to bless me, so that I may be worthy of His Mercy and His

Grace. During my stay at Dr. Coyaji Home, time and again I was ruffled by this question, is this my home? Is Dr. Coyaji Home, my home? Or is my home elsewhere?

I was assailed by many doubts. Have I lived a pure life? I ask myself, If now I pass away to another world, will I find a place at His feet? Does my life bear witness to the Lord?

One day, I feel an indefinable burden on my mind. I felt sad and morose. In that state of sorrow I told my God, 'True, I may not be worthy of your Divinity; nevertheless, my God, I thirst for you.' That was my verbal conversation with God:

> I penned down a few lines to unburden myself:
> I am guilty;
> I have plenty of shortcomings;
> Yet, I thirst for you... only you!
> I let the days go by,
> Without earning a dime,
> Yet, I thirst for you, only you.
> I did not chant your name, nor did I meditate
> Yet, my Lord, I thirst for you. I yearn for you.

•••••

Late in the night, in the silence of the hospital, I sense, the presence of someone. In the dead of the night, when everyone is fast a sleep, I hear a song from the stars, a song which is sung by a mendicant outside, in the street I experience, a vibration, I experience the presence of someone, someone who is divine and from the other world. The song is a wake-up call; All this world is an illusion.

After my discharge from Dr. Coyaji Home, on my return to my own place, I realised that world was a mere passing drama. During my stay in the hospital, some dear devotees had left this world. A dear soul in Pakistan also had passed away. Truly, the world is an illusion. It is temporary and effervescent. Day in and day out, during the morning worship and the evening prayer, these word hammer my heart. 'The world is a transient house.' I was so much with the feeling of *Vairag*, that the following words poured out of my heart:

> Where are you, Jamshed, where?
> Where are you, Oh, beautiful soul, a great brother?
> The Time has rung the death bell,
> Remember, this one thing,
> All this world is a transient place.
> Where is Jamshed, the great philanthropist?
> The great soul, who helped thousands with his Charity.
> The noble man, who served the humanity? He has left this world.

Do you know the meaning of 'Dada'? It means the elder brother. The true meaning of this word was given to me by my Guru. Dada means Giver! My Guru was truly a 'Giver'. As per the tradition, it is the disciple who serves the Master. In my case, an unusual case, the Master had served the disciple. Ruminating on this thought, I feel the pangs of separation from my Guru. Where are you, my Dada, I cry from the depths of my heart.

I hear the voices again:

> We are travellers, the traveller's Inn
> Opens the door, but where is my Home?

Remember, this spiritual talk
This world is a transitory walk.

You are a pilgrim here for days two,
Tomorrow you shall be gone,
Weep, over your sad condition,

Remember, this spiritual talk
This world is a transitory walk.

The bulbul yearns for the rose,
The colours spread in repose
Oh, beautiful One, for that one glimpse

Remember, this spiritual talk
This world is a transitory walk.

You are a bird with wings,
You fly a little you sing

Remember, this spiritual talk
This world is a transitory walk.

The image in your heart
Is a mirage
Death lurks everywhere.

Remember, this spiritual talk
This world is a transitory walk.

Your cup may be filled with joys or sorrow
Drop by drop
Everything will be erased by tomorrow.

Remember, this spiritual talk
This world is a transitory walk.

> Every moment
> The tree of life
> Sheds leaves
> This quarrel, this misery
> This turmoil
> Is of no avail
> Remember, this spiritual talk
> This world is a transitory walk.

The leaves of our life fall every day. Life is temporary, a passing phase. For this temporary sojourn, why do you waste your energies in anxiety and quarrels, Why do the nations fight and wage wars?

Every thing passes away. There is nothing permanent here.

Life truly is a puzzle. It is also a dilemma. Life is difficult to understand. What is its purpose? What is its goal? Why this panorama of joy, sorrow and turmoil?

Life is still a mystery! Time and again I have pondered over this mystery and told myself, 'Indeed life is a mystery.' It is beyond the comprehension of a rational human mind.

After returning from the Dr. Coyaji Home, I once again reflected on the mystery of life. What is life?

Life is a riddle. How do I solve this riddle?

Life is an illusion; it is an enigma! I weep as the scenario of past flashes through my mind. Life is a puzzle indeed. The dear and the near ones have flown away to another region. Things appear and disappear. There is sorrow, joy, poverty, misery, and unhappiness.

Some are basking in the glory of their success, and others are down in the dumps because of their failure; some are rolling in luxuries, and others cry for a loaf of bread. What does this mean? I find no answer. I tell myself:

> Join the vanguard of *fakirs*,
> See the illuminated path!
> Find the reality in that hour!
>
> Dirt on feet, dust on face,
> Lean and frugal, they radiate
> Light: that's life's mystery!

Some of the *fakirs*, shabbily clothed, lean, cloaked with dirt, have found the Truth: the reality of life! They have solved the puzzle!

Even Sri Ram who ate half bitten berries of Shabri, radiated light in that act of humility. God's men, *fakirs*, are humble; poor wanderers, seeking God. Blessed are those who live in humility and love; who shower their compassion on all! The life of contradictions and similarities prevails all around us, provoking us to question: what is the meaning of all this? What is the mystery? What is the reality? At this stage in my life I have realised that some secrets of life can be known, if we nurture compassion and serve the poor.

There is a famous story of the great king, whose name is Drushtant. A powerful, influential ruler, he is defeated in the war. Stripped of his mighty kingdom, he is taken as a prisoner to a jail. Just then a poor man comes to him and begs for money. The king puts his hand in the pocket and realises that he has only fifty rupees. The noble king feels, that it is below his dignity to give less than fifty rupees to the poor man! So he gives him all of fifty rupees with the word, God bless you! May you be happy.

This king has no money, but he has a rich heart.

He refuses reprieve from the prison. He lives and meets his end in the prison.

While in the prison, he writes about the mystery of life:

Love not this world,
This world betrays,
Love but one Khudha
Who stays
With you always,
Strange, strange are the ways
Of this Life!

Serve the world, but without attachment. For the world is selfish. Do not love even the power, the authority, of a royalty, because even these betray, and do not stay with you. God, alone remains with you.

Today on 25th November I realise how the years have slipped by. It was only the other day, that I took a bag of books and trotted to a Sindhi medium school to study. Many years have passed by, but God in his mercy, has always protected me and kept me by His side. Thank you God.

The Night of Awakening/Enlightment

Let me disclose a secret. 25th November is not my real Birthday. Nor is the year 1879. My true birthday falls on the night of Revelation. It happened when I was away from my native Sind.

I was taking a walk in the verandah of my house. It was a moonlit night, the silvery radiance covered the earth. The glow of the moon and the shine of the stars created a magical effect. In that glorious moment I heard a voice within me.

> Quench your thirst for God
> Be a servant of sages and saints!

On that night I was re-born. I had found the illuminated path. Since then God has been kind and merciful and has kept me in his close embrace.

Blessed is that night, for I experienced the mystical melting away of physical objects, and buildings into an infinite space.

The whole world was dissolved into the Infinite Universe. I felt a profound emptiness, without trees; without hills, rivers, and mountains – The entire world had disappeared in an Abeyance- In that space less space, I saw a flame burning bright; a spectacular light illuminated my heart. Blessed was that moment of Awakening! Since then I have seen light shinning in all: **Men, Birds and Animals.** I have witnessed the same Divinity in all the races and religions and nations of the world.

This mystical/Spiritual experience overwhelmed me. In that moment of Divine Grace, I bowed down to God and thanked Him profoundly. Since that day, my heart is filled with an ocean of love. The only cry I hear at the door of sages and saints is: Fill my cup with your Divine love.

So filled I was with the power Divine, that my body began to shiver. The moon became a symbol of Divinity. Every night thereafter, I would go to the terrace and worship the moon. For the radiance of moon glowed everything around me. I was convinced that the same light (jyot) shines in all; in everything; in you and in me. We have only to remove the veils of illusion covering us.

•••••

I love and revere trees. This intense love for trees has come, as an inspiration from my Gurudev. His love for trees was amazing. Often as I sit here in satsang hall, amongst you my devotees, my heart yearns to run and be with that tree. I want to go and hug that tree, sit under its beautiful loving shade, and take its blessings! I feel linked with the trees and through them feel deeply connected with the Nature. When I express this desire during the rainy season – for I love the rains, the soft misty drizzle enchants me – I am advised to remain indoors. It is cold outside; it is pouring, I am told. Saddened by this reply, I allow my mind to loiter around the tree, for I long for it, I love it dearly.

Shabri, (the character of a poor Bhakta from Ramayan) is very dear to my heart. The other day, devotees brought me down, and very kindly took me to the mango grove. On the way, I saw a poor old woman. I made a request to stop the car. I called out to that haggard woman, who looked pathetic in her torn dirty clothes. My heart was filled with compassion for her, and taking out a five rupee note from my pocket, I gave it to her. She is my 'Shabri', I repeated to myself.

Today is a day of reflection. My younger brother is lying unconscious in Grant's Nursing Home. Days, months, and years have passed by, and today, he is in a state of ill health, where nobody can help him. The only help, that can be sought is from the Almighty God!

Such a day will come for me too. Such a day will come for all of us; where the only refuge will be our Creator! Our Sindhi saints and poets, have described this day in their poetry and writings. Shah Abdul Latif, that great Sufi poet, who had seen the Divine Light – the Flame of Love – burning, says:

At the end of it, the world is ephemeral!

Our existence on this earth is temporary. Our lives are limited. We may think, we may live, we have thoughts, emotions, we do work and worship, but at the end of it all, it is dust. The day comes for all of us, when we have to bid good-bye and say *Khuda Hafiz, Khuda Hafiz!*

When the journey of life nears the end, what should you do? When the death lurks around your dear ones and loved ones, what should you do? Go and find a Guru, seek his teachings and blessings. Practise what he says. A famous saint, Tulsidas, talks of a 'Yoga'/union which is very easy. The 'Yoga' of '*Naam kirtan*'. *Naam Yoga* is highly exhalted in the Guru Granth Sahib. If you practise *Naam Yoga*, your end will be comfortable; and your transition to the Higher spheres smooth and painless.

What is '*Naam Yoga*'? It is the union with the Guru/ the Beloved through *Bhakti*, through *Naam Jap*. Through *Naam Simran* (through the recitation of the Holy Name) you develop devotion or *Bhakti*. *Naam Simran* is the easy way to link with Higher self. Today, we are unhappy, because of 'separateness'. We are separate from God. Our consciousness is separate from the Supreme consciousness. It is this separateness which is the cause of all sorrow. Develop equanimity. Keep your mind rooted in the One who is solid and firm. Bhagavad Gita teaches us to remain equanimous under all circumstances. We should maintain our composure in sorrow and in joy. Sri Krishna tells Arjun: One who treats joy and sorrow as equal, is my true devotee.

Life is an ocean of waves. Sometimes there are waves of joy: sometimes of sorrow. He, who is devoted to the Lord, and immersed in *Bhakti* faces ups and downs of life with equanimity. This equanimity comes from devotion: Light the lamp, the lamp of devotion.

A devotee of the Lord, a saint of our times describes it beautifully:

He is the light of my eye,
He is the love of my love;

Such a man is a true devotee of God.

God is the light of my eyes, God is the love of my heart; such is the 'Oneness' of a true *Bhakti*.

May we reach that stage of our journey where every person is an image of God: and God is the apple of our eye.

Such oneness should be our ultimate goal.

I prefer to call God as my Beloved. Who is a Beloved?? How I thirst for him; perhaps you cannot even fathom it. Beloved, loved one; My desire. My Destiny. I do not wish to disclose or describe the depth of my emotions. Perhaps, a glimpse of it can be found in the wail of a song, by a Sindhi fakir saint. I have repeated this heart wrenching phrase again and again. It describes the pathos, the pain of the poet who yearns for his Beloved.

> The sun has set in the gathering dusk.
> Yet,
> I have not met
> My Beloved.

Oh Sun, you have disappeared into the darkness of the night, but I have still not found my Beloved; I have not realized my Destiny nor I have realized my Goal! I have touched the twilight years of my life; sun has set, and yet I haven't had a glimpse of my Beloved. My days are numbered, I may fly away any moment. My journey has reached its end without meeting Him, My Beloved Lord. My search for Him is intense, my whole life has been a quest.

O Sun! When you set: Give the message to my Beloved. Take this message and be kind enough to deliver it to my Master Beloved. The message-

> Trudging miles and miles of this earthly journey, this poor creature died;
>
> She waited years and years of longing, she died waiting for you.

O Beloved, you did not meet her.

Yearning for you, waiting, she died heart broken.

Oh Beloved, every moment, every breath is filled with longing for you. Every place, every nook and corner, every space, I search for your face; every step I take, there is a hope, you may cross my path and I may find you, by my side – in din of noise, in silence of my heart, there is but one cry- cry of my soul:

My Beloved, why are you so far!

My soul wails- hold me close to your heart, my beloved.

Bless me, devotees, that I may be united with my Beloved, that I should quench my thirst for Him; that I should meet my Beloved face to face. I am fortunate to have his vision; I am blessed to be at his Lotus feet. But His face is yet not revealed to me fully. May be I have still a long way to go; may be I am not worthy of such Divinity. It is, His kindness, His grace, that he has given me a place at His Lotus feet. But I long for the veils to be lifted. I yearn to see His luminous Face.

Man is surrounded by veils. There are many veils. According to some there are as many as 70 veils. May these veils be removed- and the Beauteous Face of my Beloved be revealed.

Bless me, my dear ones, that I may see that day before my death- When my Beloved will reveal His face, will slate my thirst with His Divine love. And bless me with His benign look.

Death Song

Come hither my fellow beings,
Come, O' children of my beloved motherland!
Grant me your blessings / As I bid you good bye,
The call has come from spaces blue,
Farewell, O friends! Good-bye, Adieu,
God be with you.

You have sailed into my dreams, again and again
My Beloved, My friend will surely,
Lighten your grief,
Your sorrow,
The call has come……..

My boat is ready at the wharf,
It's time to sail, to cross the sand bars,
Come and bless me lest I may delay, the onward march,
The curtain has fallen,
Life's drama has come to an end,
I need good wishes of each of my friends,
The call has come……..

With roses red and flowers white,
I have gazed into life, with golden light,
Come, fill your cup with that love Divine,
Give me a bit, before I vanish into Gleaming line,
The call has come.........

The beautiful gifts of life, I carry to the world beyond,
Be assured, I shall return from that Native shore,
To serve the suffering human hearts,
Even the birds, animals, and the stars / and light their path,
For I aspire not for, salvation, nor for Moksh,
My yearning is to be dust,
A dot and no more,
With these gifts, my boat sails ashore
To the kingdom of Christ, who pours
His Divine grace
To the beautiful realm of Krishna
Where love vibrates into light,
The call has come..........